T5-CRC-380

LIVINGSTON

AND THE

TOMATO

LIVINGSTON

AND THE

TOMATO

A. W. LIVINGSTON

WITH

A FOREWORD AND AN APPENDIX

BY

ANDREW F. SMITH

OHIO STATE UNIVERSITY PRESS
COLUMBUS

Illustrations appearing in the gallery courtesy of Alan W. Livingston and
James R. Huber. Frontispiece illustration courtesy of James R. Huber.

Foreword and Appendix © 1998 by Andrew F. Smith.

All rights reserved.

Library of Congress Cataloging-in-Publication Data
Livingston, A. W. (Alexander W.), 1822–1898.
Livingston and the tomato / A.W. Livingston ; with a foreword and
appendix by Andrew F. Smith
p.   cm.
Originally published: Columbus, Ohio : A.W. Livingston's Sons,
1893. With a new foreword and appendix.
Includes bibliographical references (p.   ) and index.
ISBN 0-8142-5009-2
(pa : alk. paper)
1. Tomatoes.   2. Tomatoes—Varieties.   3. Livingston, A. W.
(Alexander W.), 1822–1898.   I. Smith, Andrew F., 1946–
II. Title
SB349.L78   1998
635'.642—dc21   98-4410
CIP

Cover design by Diane Gleba Hall.

Printed by Thomson-Shore.

The paper used in this publication meets
the minimum requirements of the American
National Standard for Information Sciences—
Permanence of Paper for Printed Library Materials.
ANSI Z39.48-1992.

9 8 7 6 5 4 3 2 1

CONTENTS

FOREWORD

A NY TOMATO AFFICIONADO would be delighted to see the sign bearing the inscription "Birthplace of the Tomato" greeting those who enter Reynoldsburg, a small town about twelve miles east of Columbus, Ohio. This boast was founded on the work of Alexander W. Livingston, a tomato seedsman born in Reynoldsburg, who developed and promoted more enduring tomato varieties than any other American during the nineteenth century. In addition, the seed company he and his sons founded contributed more to the development of the tomato before World War II than did any other source.

Alexander Livingston's contributions might well have been lost save for the publication of his book *Livingston and the Tomato,* delineating his achievements in improving the tomato. Looking back over the century since its publication, we can see that *Livingston and the Tomato* was much more than merely a vanity publication or an advertising gimmick. It was, in fact, the first comprehensive book about tomatoes published in America, chronicling the rapid conversion of the tomato from what was a ribbed, hard-cored, frequently hollow fruit to the delicious, juicy, lip-smacking fruit we know and love today. The late nineteenth century was a period of vast growth for tomato culture in Ohio and throughout the United States, and *Livingston and the Tomato* directly concerns itself with this crucial period in the tomato's history. It also, however, offers insight into life in that period of Ohio, and America's history. Alexander Livingston's pioneering work, his entrepreneurial sons who transformed his efforts into a successful business concern, their expansive far-flung operations, the application of scientific principles to agricultural practices, and the mammoth growth of the canning and preserving industries were all reflections of the spirit of Ohio and America at the cusp of the twentieth century.

The Tomato in Ohio

Ohio's first contact with the tomato predated Alexander Livingston's birth by only a few decades. When the first Europeans arrived in what is today Ohio, they found no tomatoes (which are known by the genus and species name of *Lycopersicon esculentum*). Although the tomato had originated in the New World before the arrival of the Spanish conquistadors, it had been cultivated only in Mexico and Central America. During the mid-sixteenth and early seventeenth centuries, the Spanish introduced tomatoes into what is today the United States when forming settlements in Florida. They also cultivated them in New Orleans during their period of control, as the French may also have done previously. From Florida, tomatoes slowly migrated northward along the Atlantic coast. Tomatoes were cultivated in seventeenth-century South Carolina, and ample evidence has been uncovered to indicate they were consumed by southerners during the eighteenth century. From New Orleans, tomatoes spread up the Mississippi River system, reaching Ohio around the beginning of the nineteenth century.[1] Simultaneously, tomatoes were probably also brought into Ohio by early settlers from Virginia and the Carolinas.

In a letter of 1871, Thomas Ewing, a U.S. senator from Ohio and the holder of two cabinet posts, recalled a rural scene dating the appearance of the tomato in Ohio to as early as the summer of 1800, when a certain Mrs. Brown planted a tomato plant. The children were playing in the garden, he told, "when suddenly the alarm was raised, and ran through the little group, that Apphia Brown had eaten a love-apple. We sped with the fearful intelligence to the grown up-people, who did not partake of our alarm, and it passed off without a catastrophe." Despite the tomato's early appearance in Ohio, however, many years passed before Ewing saw tomatoes used for culinary purposes.[2]

A U.S. senator from Illinois and a judge, Jesse Thomas recalled that his wife had been introduced to tomato cookery by Francis Vigo in Vincennes, Indiana, in the late eighteenth century. In 1807 she grew tomatoes in her garden in Lawrenceburg, Indiana, and from Lawrenceburg, Thomas believed, tomatoes were introduced to Cincinnati, Ohio. Shortly thereafter, evidence shows, tomatoes were being cultivated in Cincinnati. A man named John H. James raised tomatoes in his garden in Cincinnati in 1813, and he reported that they were sold in markets at least as early as 1816. Indeed, Jared

Mansfield, U.S. Surveyor General of the Northwest Terri-
tories, was so impressed with Cincinnati tomatoes that
he sent seeds to friends in Wallingford, Connecticut. An
Ohio receipt book of the period included two recipes for
tomato sauce. During the 1820s and early 1830s tomatoes were mentioned regularly in Cincinnati farming and
gardening periodicals. Also during the early 1830s, the
British author Frances Trollope, mother of Anthony Trollope, visited Ohio and reported that tomatoes were "the
great luxury of the American table in the opinion of most
Europeans." In Cincinnati, she found tomatoes to be "in
the highest perfection in the market for about sixpence a
peck," available from June to December.[3]

Despite the tomato's cultivation in southern Ohio,
many Ohioans eschewed the fruit as late as the 1830s.
Martin Welker reported that in central Ohio the tomato
was "laid upon the mantel for an ornament, with the
mother's injunction that it was poisonous and must not
be eaten." Alexander Livingston's mother gave similar
advice in 1832: "You must not eat them, my child. They
must be poison, for even the hogs will not eat them."[4]

Similar distrustful beliefs were espoused by other
Americans, particularly in the northern states. However,
more significant—if mundane—reasons emerged as to
why Americans shunned tomatoes. Some found that the
smell of the plant itself made them nauseous, and some
Americans believed that this odor served as warning
against consumption of its fruit. Others did not like the
tomato's appearance. One gardener stated that the first
time he saw tomatoes they "appeared so disgusting that

I thought I must be very hungry before I should be induced to taste them." The look of the tomato was so disagreeable that many people supposed it would "never receive a permanent place in our list of culinary vegetables." Likewise, many people found the tomato disagreeable to taste. During the late 1820s, J. B. Garber posited that "hardly two persons in a hundred, on first tasting it, thought that they would ever be induced to taste that *sour trash* a second time." A writer in the *Genesee Farmer* said that the tomato was offensive in whatever shape it was offered, while a writer in the *Horticulturist* described tomatoes as "odious and repulsive smelling berries." Even these hostile judgments paled in comparison to those of Joseph T. Buckingham, editor of the *Boston Courier*, who called tomatoes "the mere fungus of an offensive plant, which one cannot touch without an immediate application of soap and water with an infusion of *eau de cologne,* to sweeten the hand—tomatoes, the twin-brothers to soured and putrescent potato-balls—deliver us, O ye caterers of luxuries, ye gods and goddesses of the science of cookery! deliver us from tomatoes."[5]

Tomato Mania

American views toward the tomato were transformed during the 1830s, largely through the efforts of two Ohioans: John Cook Bennett and Archibald Miles. Born in Massachusetts in 1804, Bennett lived much of his early life in southeastern Ohio. A medical doctor by profession, Bennett immersed himself in the study of plants and their medicinal effects. In 1834 he read a Cincinnati

newspaper article announcing that tomatoes, "a delight-
ful vegetable," were selling in the market at the extrava-
gant price of fifty cents per dozen. The article reported
that tomatoes could be "raised with less than half the
trouble and expense that attend the growing of cucumbers" and were "a much hardier and more prolific plant."
The writer urged their cultivation, reassuring his readers
that tomatoes had "an acid flavor, which, by use, becomes
agreeable to most persons, although not always relished
when first tasted." While green tomatoes made good pickles, when ripened they could be used in soups, hashes,
stews, confections, and ketchups. The wholesomeness of
the tomato, the author believed, was "a subject properly
belonging to the medical faculty."[6]

Shortly after reading the article, Bennett became
the president of the medical department of Willoughby
University of Lake Erie in Chagrin (later renamed Willoughby), Ohio. In his opening lecture of November 1834,
Bennett reported that tomatoes successfully treated di-
arrhea, violent bilious attacks, and dyspepsia (indiges-
tion) and prevented cholera. Bennett urged all citizens to
eat tomatoes, as they were "the most healthy article of
the Materia Alimentary." Bennett left Willoughby in
March 1835 and shortly thereafter published an article
restating these claims in the *Ohio Farmer and Western
Horticulturist*. This article was reprinted in August and
September of that year in the *Cincinnati Daily Gazette*,
the *Daily Cleveland Herald*, the *Ohio State Journal and
Columbus Gazette*, the *Marietta Gazette*, and in literally
hundreds of other newspapers and periodicals through-

out the United States. Two years later, Bennett moved to New Athens, where he published a series of articles on the tomato's history, culture, hygiene, uses, chemical composition, and varieties. Bennett's views were reprinted for decades in medical journals, newspapers, and gardening and agricultural periodicals, not only in the United States but also eventually in Australia, the United Kingdom, and France.[7]

Bennett's effusive claims won over many people, the most important of whom was Archibald Miles. Miles's family had moved to Cleveland shortly after his birth in New York in 1804. He briefly studied medicine before deciding upon a career as a merchant. In 1824 he opened up the first general store in Brunswick, strategically located on the turnpike between Cleveland and Columbus. Like many merchants, in addition to selling goods Archibald Miles sold drugs. During the 1830s he became an agent for "British Hygiene," a "restorative" medicine developed in Great Britain, and in 1836 he marketed "American Hygiene Pills," a product of his own creation. He then met a physician, thought to have been Dr. John Cook Bennett, who suggested that he change the name to "extract of tomato" because of the medical profession's interest in the medicinal virtues of the tomato.[8]

Miles moved to Cincinnati in the spring of 1837, and in July he launched "Dr. Miles' Compound Extract of Tomato." According to his advertisements, these pills cured dyspepsia, headaches, intermittent and remittent fevers, "ill-conditioned ulcers, hepatic and other cuticular affections, hepatitis, complaints of the liver, local congestions, bilious colic," "all complaints requiring an aperient," and "glandular and other concealed affections of the skin." For children this medicine "cured Summer Complaint, Whooping Cough, Measles," and many other diseases. While Miles did not claim that his tomato pills cured all diseases, he did maintain that there was "no *one* medicine that will succeed more frequently." By late 1837 his pills were advertised in almost every part of the country. In addition to advertisements, favorable articles about Miles's pills were published in journals and newspapers in Ohio.[9]

The success of the campaign on behalf of "Dr. Miles' Compound Extract of Tomato" was immediate. An estimated one hundred thousand people reportedly consumed tomato pills throughout the United States and the Carribean in the late 1830s. Success, however, brought competition and scrutiny from the medical community. By 1840 "every variety of pill and panacea" was composed of "extract of tomato," but despite their early success, tomato pills were widely discredited as a hoax, and the national market collapsed in the early 1840s.[10] However, most observers admitted that the tomato was a healthy esculent even if they disagreed with the enthusiastic assertions of the pill vendors.

While cultivation of the tomato increased slowly before the tomato pill outburst, a tomato craze swept Ohio and the nation during the late 1830s and early 1840s, and the culinary use of the tomato expanded rapidly. Edward Hooper, the editor of Cincinnati's *Western Farmer and Gardener,* included three recipes for preserving tomatoes and two recipes for tomatoes and beefsteak in his publication in 1839. Hooper's *Practical Farmer, Gardener and Housewife* in 1842 featured recipes for tomato sauce, tomato omelet, beef à la daub (with tomatoes), tomato ham, tomato ketchup, and two types of tomato soup, as well as several techniques for preserving and drying tomatoes. Lettice Bryan's *The Kentucky Housewife*, published in Cincinnati in 1841, incorporated tomatoes in various recipes such as okra soup, gumbo, tomato soup, tomato sauce, green tomato pickles, baked tomatoes, broiled tomatoes, stewed tomatoes, tomato jumbles, fried tomatoes, tomato soy, tomato jelly, and tomato marmalade. She featured two recipes for tomato ketchup and three recipes for preserving tomatoes. That same year George Girardey's *Manual of Domestic Economy,* published in Dayton, Ohio, contained six tomato recipes, including ones for sauce and marmalade. In the following year he translated his manual into German and published it in Cincinnati as *Höchst nützliches Handbuch über Kochkunst,* the first German-language cookbook published in the United States.[11]

Edward Hooper reported in 1842 that, because of the curative claims, the price of tomatoes had doubled, and he predicted that their consumption would soon quadruple. One farmer growing tomatoes in Cincinnati, Hooper said, had made a thousand dollars in a single summer.[12] Needless to say, this was a small fortune by the standards of the day. During the late 1840s and 1850s, almost every cookbook and gardening and agricultural periodical published in Ohio included tomato recipes or other references.

The tomato's rise to prominence before 1860 was

dwarfed by the subsequent dramatic increase in its cultivation and consumption. During the Civil War camp
cooks served Ohio's soldiers tomato omelets. Tomatoes
were being canned in Cincinnati by 1860, and the canning industry expanded exponentially after the Civil
War.[13]

Tomato Varieties

Despite the expansion of tomato consumption before the
Civil War, up to this point there had been relatively little
change in the tomato itself. The original tomato fruit was
two-celled; pre-Columbian Amerindians developed a tomato with a large, lumpy, multicelled fruit; and Meso-
americans nurtured and developed other variations. By
the time mainstream Americans cultivated tomatoes, the
fruit came in a wide variety of shapes, sizes, and colors.
However, despite this extensive diversity, the *American
Agriculturist* maintained in 1848 that in the United
States few varieties were esteemed: these were the large
smooth-skinned red, common red, pear-shaped, and
cherry varieties. A nascent relationship already existed
between tomato varieties and their culinary usage. Red tomatoes, for instance, were thought best for ketchup and
cooking. Fig-shaped tomatoes were frequently recommended for making confections. Pear-shaped, cherry-
shaped, and yellow types were employed for pickling.[14]

Before the Civil War, farmers began saving seeds
to produce new tomato varieties. In Rochester, New York,
J. Slater reserved seeds from the roundest and smoothest
tomatoes he could find. Slater claimed that his tomatoes

were neither flat nor wrinkled "but as round as an orange, and as smooth and large as the largest Northern
Spy apple." Unfortunately, his tomatoes seem to have
disappeared before they could be commercialized by
seedsmen.[15]

At the same time that American farmers were at-
tempting to produce improved varieties of tomatoes, new
varieties were being imported into the United States from
France, the United Kingdom, and other countries. This
effort dramatically increased the gene pool. One imported tomato was a variety purportedly brought back
from the Pacific in 1841. The *U.S. Gazette* reported that
the American Exploring Expedition in the South Pacific
had run across what they called the Fejee tomato. A sailor
sent Fejee seeds back to a friend in Philadelphia, while
Charles Wilkes, the captain of the expedition, dispatched
them to the secretary of the navy, James Pauling, who
evidently dispersed them. These Fejee seeds had no discernible effect on tomato culture and apparently disappeared after a few years of cultivation. This name, *Fejee,*
was later incorrectly applied to another variety popular
after the Civil War.[16]

Farmers and gardeners used newly introduced varieties and slowly bred other tomatoes in the quest to develop round, smooth-skinned fruit with solid flesh. Writing in the *Horticulturist,* William Chorlton noted that if
agricultural societies and fairs rewarded these characteristics, the standards for tomato quality would rise.
The large growers would soon be "forced to take a better
sample to the city, instead of the thick skinned, hollow

subjects, which are too often seen on the huckster's stall, which 'bounce' like a foot-ball."[17]

The benefits of these breeding efforts first became apparent just before the Civil War. Fearing Burr's *Field and Garden Vegetables of America,* initially published in 1863, reflected Burr's experience as a seedsman and gardener in Massachusetts during the late 1850s. He listed twenty-two tomato varieties, only one of which is not now considered to fall within the *Lycopersicon* genus. The 1865 edition of his book listed two additional varieties.[18]

In 1858 Henry Tilden of Davenport, Iowa, discovered a tomato growing in a field: it was solid and prolific, but dwarf. He christened it the Tilden tomato. In 1864 Tilden claimed to have grossed six hundred dollars from the sale of only one acre's worth of his new variety's fruit. It was better than other varieties on the market at the time, and it was released to the public the next year by seedsman Apollos W. Harrison of Philadelphia. Of the Tilden tomato, a writer in *American Gardening* said, "It was red, inclined to grow long fruited, smooth and without seams or creases, large, but not so early as Cook's Favorite, but much more strong." The Cook's Favorite had been introduced in 1864, with a fruit of "peach-like form, very thick between the blossom and the stem ends, red, free from open cells, smooth exterior, but only of second size." Ten years later, the Cook's Favorite was rechristened the Canada Victor.[19]

In 1862 a new Fejee tomato (also called Fiji Island or Beefsteak) was first offered in the seed catalogues. Despite its name, it was probably was an import from Italy.

Wherever its source, its qualities were unequaled in the
United States. The fruit was a large, solid, rough, very
heavy, productive, purple-skinned sort. Seedsman Burnet
Landreth of Pennsylvania believed that the Fejee was the
ancestor of all other purple sorts, including Livingston's
Acme and Livingston's Beauty. ("Purple" used in reference to tomatoes means a deep red or a pink color.)[20]
   By far the most successful tomato variety, however,
was developed by Dr. T. J. Hand, originally from Sing
Sing, New York. During the 1850s he began crossing the
small cherry tomato with several larger lumpy varieties.
His efforts were rewarded when he produced a tomato
with a solid mass of flesh and juice, small seeds, and
smooth skin. Under the name Trophy tomato, it experienced unbounded success after the Civil War. Its pro-
moter, Colonel George E. Waring, sold seeds for twenty-
five cents apiece.[21] The Trophy was better than other varieties at the time, but far more important was Waring's
demonstration that it was possible to make a fortune selling tomato varieties. This encouraged others, including
Alexander Livingston, to redouble their efforts to breed
new varieties.

Alexander W. Livingston

Alexander Livingston's parents, John and Mary Graham
Livingston, were married in Cambridge, New York. In
1815 they moved to Reynoldsburg, Ohio, and six years
later, in 1821, Alexander was born. He grew up in Reynoldsburg. At the age of twenty-one he began working for
a seed grower in the area, and two years later he married

Matilda Graham. Their marriage of forty-six years resulted in ten children, all living to adulthood except the
firstborn, John, who died at the age of two. To support
his family, Livingston leased property and began farming, and by 1852 he had saved enough to purchase land.
In 1856 Livingston purchased four hundred consignment boxes of the Buckeye Garden Seed Company
from Robert Robertson, a seedsman who moved to Iowa.
The consignment sales of his garden seeds increased extensively, allowing Livingston to purchase additional
land and leases. Farmers would bring their crops to the
company, and their fruit was weighed and paid for by the
ton. The company stripped the skin and flesh off the tomato and placed the mush into a hopper and a crusher.
The mush was then run through a screen that moved the
seeds into a vat, where they molded. These seeds were
eventually washed and placed into an Osnaburg bag made
of linen or cotton (to let water out). The bag was wrung
dry, and the seeds removed and dried by fans. Livingston
sold the seeds to merchants on a consignment basis. From
1864 to 1865 he built a home, consolidating the farming
and seed operations into one location. The house is now
owned by the city of Reynoldsburg and managed under
the care of the Livingston House Society, founded in
1992.[22]
    By 1848 Livingston had experimented not only with
tomatoes but with many different plants. His aim for tomatoes in particular was to produce a plant with fruit
"smooth in contour, uniform in size, and better flavored."
Livingston tried the best tomato varieties then available.

He grew each variety, saved seeds from the best specimens, planted them during the following season, and observed the results. Even with his careful cultivation, this
process engendered only small improvements; the seed of
each succession produced fruit similar to the original.
After fifteen years, his tomatoes still bore fruit that was
"thin-fleshed, rough and undesirable."[23]

Other growers were more successful. New tomato
varieties—the previously mentioned Fejee, Cook's Favorite, Tilden, and the Trophy—were released by other
seedsmen. Livingston experimented with these varieties,
but again was not rewarded with success, and so in 1865
he tried a different method: plant selection. In managing
his tomato fields he sought out plants distinctly different
from what he planted. He found one plant with heavy foliage that produced a prolific, uniformly round fruit. Unfortunately, the fruit was too small for commercial use.
He saved the seed from this plant and cultivated two rows
during the following spring. Of this crop, he carefully
harvested the seed from the first ripe and best specimens.
During the following years the fruit "took on flesh, size
and improved qualities." After five years of work, Livingston was satisfied with his product and marketed it under
the name of Livingston's Paragon. Its fruit was larger
than many of the standard tomato varieties then available. According to Livingston, it "was the first perfectly
and uniformly smooth tomato ever introduced to the
American public, or, so far as I have ever learned, the first
introduced to the world."[24]

Whether the Paragon was the first tomato variety to

be uniformly smooth and round was challenged by many, but what was indisputable was its popularity. The Paragon quickly became a favorite among market gardeners and canners and was sold by many other seedsmen. In 1883 a reader in the *Gardener's Monthly* proclaimed that the Paragon was almost perfect. In 1886—sixteen years after its introduction—the editor of the *American Agriculturist* reported that the Paragon "in beauty, solidity, regular form and excellent quality . . . is the best tomato currently available." According to a major competitor, the Landreth Seed Company in Pennsylvania, the Paragon was "the perfection of a Tomato—large, solid and smooth as an Apple, and deep red." They believed it was a superb variety, for which "no praise can be too high." Of course, Landreth neglected to mention that the Paragon had been developed by Livingston.[25]

Seventeen years after the Paragon was first introduced, the renowned botanist Liberty Hyde Bailey reported that it was "constant in size and shape, three to four inches across and two inches deep, usually perfectly regular when ripe, bright light red, firm, and good." It continued to be marketed for seven decades after its initial introduction, a remarkable feat for any variety. In addition, other seedsmen grew the Paragon, renamed their results, and sold them as new varieties: Bailey reported he could find no difference between the Paragon and other varieties subsequently sold under the names of New Jersey, Arlington, Emery, Autocrat, Mayflower, and Scoville.[26]

While developing the Paragon constituted a large

stride toward creating a perfectly round tomato, the fruit was of medium size and was an early ripener. Livingston continued seeking other unusual tomatoes that might overcome these characteristics. He found one plant with fruit that ripened early, had solid flesh, was of medium size, slightly oval, but smooth-skinned. Its color was maroon or red with a slight tinge of purple. Livingston developed this plant just as he had developed the Paragon, and in 1875 he released it under the name of Livingston's Acme. According to Landreth, it was "a popular sort everywhere" and "of superlative merit."[27] Another seedsman, Robert Buist, reported that the Acme was

> an entirely distinct character, and has become a very popular variety; it is perfection in its BEAUTY, SOLIDITY and EARLINESS, and has good carrying qualities, a very important requisite for a desirable market variety; it is also well adapted for Southern culture, and one of the best to grow for the Northern market. The plants are of a strong and vigorous growth, very productive; fruit of medium size, large enough for any use, form perfect, round, slightly depressed at the ends, very smooth; color a glossy dark red, with a sort of purplish tinge; ripens all over and through at the same time; bears continuously until frost; delicious in flavor, has no green core, and but few seeds; unequaled for canning, preserving or slicing.

According to Bailey, the Acme was one of the best varieties in cultivation. Other seedsmen favored it so much that they released "new" varieties indistinguishable from the Acme, including the Rochester, Rochester Favorite, Climax, and Essex Hybrid.[28]

Not everyone, however, was happy with the Acme. A writer in the *Gardener's Monthly* wrote, "I have from time to time cultivated most if not all the principal varieties of

tomatoes, and no variety has proved to be so subject to
the rot as the Acme. I have also found the fruit very soft
and watery when fully ripe. On this account I do not think
that it could be carried safely to any distance. Its peculiar
color, pinkish red, is decidedly objected to by many persons." Although many defended the variety, another observer wrote, "I want no more of the Acme tomato; they
rot badly."[29]

Livingston located a sport in one of his Acme tomato
fields. Its fruit was uniformly smooth and blood-red in
color. Its particular advantage was that it had a thick,
tough skin. The fruit also began to show ripening several
days early, which meant that growers could pick and ship
the fruit several days before it was fully ripe, making this
an excellent shipping tomato. Livingston introduced it in
1880 and called it Livingston's Perfection. A writer in the
New York Tribune examined several varieties of tomatoes
and concluded that Livingston's Perfection was most de-
serving of praise.[30] Although some growers reported that
the Perfection was frequently indistinguishable from the
Acme, it continued to be sold until 1922.

Like many other businesses in America, Livingston's Buckeye Garden Seed Company went bankrupt in
the crash of 1875–76. Livingston discontinued the commission business, and a new company was organized by
his son Robert. They operated under the new name of
"A. W. Livingston's Sons," although the words "The
Buckeye Garden Seed Company" continued to appear for
many years on the covers of their seed catalogues. Wide
area marketing was conducted through catalogue sales

and advertising in leading farm journals, newspapers, and gardening magazines. In 1880 the business moved from Reynoldsburg to Columbus, Ohio. Alexander Livingston himself moved to Des Moines, where he purchased a farm from his old friend Robert Robertson. In Iowa, Livingston established a site for a new company, planning to move the entire seed company from Ohio, but under his son's management the business in Columbus prospered.

A man named Harrison Crosby of Jamestown, New Jersey, was one of the first to can tomatoes, beginning in 1848. The industry grew slowly during the 1850s, but during the Civil War the war department in Washington let many canning contracts to feed the Union forces, and the tomato canning industry took off. Business expanded even more after the war, and by 1892 more than three million cans of tomatoes were produced annually. Not just any tomato could be canned, however; growers needed tomatoes with particular qualities. Out of a field of Paragons, Livingston located what he believed would be a good specimen for canning. After improving it, he introduced the tomato in 1883 as Livingston's Favorite. It was an early, blood red, smooth, and prolific tomato which ripened evenly. It was solid, meaty, and large. Livingston's catalogue claimed that the Favorite was "the *largest, perfect-shaped* Red Tomato in cultivation, smoother than the Paragon, does not crack or rot like the Acme; is a darker red than the Perfection; ripens evenly and as early as any good sort, holding its size to the end of the season; very prolific, good flavor, few seeds, flesh

solid, bears shipping long distances." W. E. Robinson &
Brother, a tomato canner in Aberdeen, Maryland, was so
impressed with Livingston's Favorite that he ordered ten
pounds of seed—which at 1,500 seeds per ounce came to
a total of 240,000 seeds.[31]

According to Livingston, canners were also seeking
a purple-colored tomato. Livingston found one growing
in a Paragon tomato patch and developed it, in 1886
christening it the Beauty. Its fruit was large and showy;
its color was deep red with a slight tone of purple. It grew
in a cluster and was "solid and meaty, smooth and free
from rot or green core," according to a Landreth seed
catalogue (which again failed to mention that Alexander
Livingston had developed the variety). By 1893 Livingston was selling 2¼ tons of Beauty seed to his own customers, while other seedsmen were marketing even more
of the varieties he had developed. A writer in *Garden and
Forest* acclaimed the Beauty as the best purple variety. In
1887 Livingston introduced another purple variety called
the Potato Leaf, whose leaves resembled those of the
Irish potato plant. Livingston considered this the best
purple tomato variety for canning. After its release Livingston concluded he had been so successful that "there
was very little opportunity left for improvement in tomatoes," admitting there was less difference between the
first tomato that he introduced and his subsequent
ones.[32]

Livingston also worked with yellow varieties. While
wandering through a county fair, he saw an attractive yellow tomato. The owner gave one to Livingston, who pre-

served the seed, tested, and improved it. In 1882 Livingston decided to release it under the name Golden Queen. It was uniformly round, golden yellow in color, with a slight tendency to be reddish at the bottom. Ripening early, and a prolific plant, it was reportedly the most flavorful tomato on the market. *Livingston's Seed Annual* touted it as "none better for slicing or preserving. Sliced with one of the red sorts it makes a pleasing appearance."[33] The Golden Queen is one of the few Livingston varieties to have been sold continuously since its introduction, although there is some question whether the current seeds sold under that name replicate the fruit of the original plant. Another variety, Livingston's Gold Ball, was found by one of the company's growers. Introduced in 1892 as a "new and improved" version of the yellow egg or plum tomato, it was used mainly for pickling and preserves. The Gold Ball was a bright golden yellow color, round, 1½ inches in diameter, with few seeds, and very productive.

Livingston was always on the lookout for new varieties with unique characteristics. In 1885 he obtained a specimen from a market gardener near Columbus that appeared particularly promising. It produced a thick, solid, red fruit shaped like the Beauty and the Favorite. Livingston continued his experiments and released it in 1889. Since the fruit weighed more than any of his other varieties, he called it the New Stone. It was subsequently used to develop several other important twentieth-century varieties, including the Earliana, Globe, and Greater Baltimore.

In 1887 Livingston introduced the Royal Red, found in Dwarf Champion fields. It was bright scarlet red in color and was used particularly in the manufacture of ketchup. Three tomatoes were introduced during the following year: Livingston's Buckeye State, the largest uniformly round tomato variety on the market; the New Dwarf Aristocrat, so named because of the plant's "erect bearing and dressy appearance"; and Livingston's Large Rose Peach tomato, a large, mild-tasting fruit that appeared resistant to tomato rot.[34]

Many of Livingston's varieties were sold by other seedsmen. A. W. Livingston's Sons also reported that large quantities of seed were being saved from the refuse of canning factories and sold as Livingston's, costing half the price of authentic Livingston seeds. The company adorned every seed package with a True Blue Seal, which guaranteed genuine seeds.

Livingston's Tomato Book

After the death of his wife in 1890, Alexander Livingston turned over his Iowa seed business to another son, Josiah, returned to Ohio, and began working on his book *Livingston and the Tomato.* Several works devoted solely to tomatoes had already been published. The first booklet, *Tomatoes from Seed to the Table,* was authored by F. F. Smith of Aurora, Illinois, in 1876, but it was simply instructional. In 1885 D. Cummins of Conneaut, Ohio, who had made a thousand dollars in one season on one acre of land growing tomatoes for canning, issued a pamphlet titled *Growing Tomatoes for Canning-Factories.* During

the 1890s a spate of tomato pamphlets appeared. J. W.
Day in Crystal Springs, Mississippi, released a short
monograph on how to grow tomatoes for export to northern cities. Alexander Livingston knew Day and even
quoted from his book in *Livingston and the Tomato.*

Amos Ives Root of Medina, Ohio—a publisher, editor, merchant, and competing seedsman—liked Day's
and Cummins's pamphlets and decided to reprint revised
versions of them along with his own article "How to Support a Family on One-Fourth Acre of Ground." Root's
Tomato Culture was published in late 1892 as a light promotional booklet for his company. Perhaps because it
was a promotional book it made no mention of Root's
competitor, Alexander Livingston, or the tomato varieties
he had developed. Root was well aware of Alexander Livingston's work, as his seed business sold the Golden
Queen, Beauty, New Stone, and the Buckeye State.[35] Livingston's absence from Root's work may well have encouraged Livingston to complete his own book.

According to his introduction, Livingston's purpose
in writing the book was to relate his experiences to seedsmen, growers, and canners about the proper cultivation,
processing, and consumption of tomatoes. The book was
published by A. W. Livingston's Sons and sold for one dollar. Customers received a free copy if they purchased ten
dollars' worth of seed; if they purchased less than ten dollars' worth, they could acquire the book at ten cents less
for every dollar they purchased.

Livingston and the Tomato was far more than just
a public relations ploy. It includes extensive information

about Alexander Livingston, his methods and results, and his ideas on how to cultivate tomatoes and how to respond to diseases and pests. In addition, Livingston's book features more than sixty tomato recipes, the largest collection of tomato recipes then assembled. Included are recipes for slicing, frying, scalloping, baking, and broiling tomatoes, for making tomato toast, custard, soup, pie, preserves, figs, jam, butter, salad, sauce, omelets, soys, ketchups, and mustards, among many other uses. Many recipes had been previously published, and a few were particularly unusual. (A recipe for French tomato pickles, for instance, was from "Mrs. President R. B. Hayes.") Livingston encouraged readers to experiment with other methods of preparing tomatoes. If these proved valuable, he urged readers to send in more recipes, promising to include them in the next edition of the book. Unfortunately, it was never published.

Alexander Livingston's Last Tomatoes

Livingston may have completed his book, but his zeal for introducing new tomatoes did not wane. The Honor Bright was discovered in a field of New Stone tomatoes in 1894 and introduced in 1897. It was promoted as different "from every other type of tomato"—its fruit, at first light green, turned to a waxy white, then lemon, and finally a rich, bright red. Rated as a superb table tomato, it was believed by some to be the best canning tomato available in the United States. The editor of the *Rural New Yorker* considered the Honor Bright to be the only tomato that could be shipped to England from the United

States without spoiling. The Dwarf Yellow Prince, released the year Livingston died, was the last of his lifetime. It matured very early and was solid-fleshed, used for ornamental purposes by slicing it along with red and purple varieties. Livingston spent the final years of his life in Columbus, where he died on November 11, 1898. The *Elmer Times* gave tribute to Alexander Livingston, saying he would "never be forgotten in the scientific agricultural world as the creator of the modern type of large, smooth tomatoes, which supercede the repulsive, twisted 'tomats' of our grandfather's time."[36]

The Livingston Seed Company

As a result of the death of one of Alexander Livingston's sons, the company incorporated in September of 1898, two months before Livingston's death. Its name was changed to the Livingston Seed Company. It prospered under the control of his sons and grandsons, who continued to develop new tomato varieties. Twentieth-century varieties included the Magnus (1900); the Dwarf Stone (1902); the Globe (1906), a cross between Livingston's New Stone and the Ponderosa; the Hummer (1907); and the Coreless (1908). In 1917 a horticulturalist in the U.S. Department of Agriculture crossed the Globe with the Marvel—a French variety—and the union produced the Marglobe, released in 1925. The Marglobe was in turn combined with the J.T.D. variety to create the Rutgers tomato. In all, the Livingstons introduced thirty-one varieties of tomatoes.

The U.S. Department of Agriculture's 1937 *Year-*

book listed A. W. Livingston as a leader in the commercial breeding of tomatoes, calling him and his colleagues "geniuses at selecting and perpetuating superior tomatoes." Victor Boswell, the principal horticulturalist at USDA's Bureau of Plant Industry, claimed that the work of Livingston and his successors "resulted in the introduction of more new varieties than that of any other private group." Of the forty tomatoes that had attained a distinct status before 1910, "a third were productions of or introductions by the Livingston Company." By 1937, Boswell estimated, "half of the major varieties were due to the abilities of the Livingstons to evaluate and perpetuate superior material in the tomato."[37]

By the 1930s the tomato seed business had undergone a major change. Before the passage of the Pure Food and Drug Act in 1907, the Livingston Seed Company processed seeds, collected the pulp, and transported it in railroad cars to the H. J. Heinz Company in Pittsburgh, where it was used in the manufacture of ketchup. To prevent fermentation of the tomato pulp, benzoate of soda was added as a preservative. After the passage of the Pure Food and Drug Act, Heinz gave up using preservatives, including benzoate of soda. This required Heinz to grow or contract farmers for tomatoes around canning factories. As ketchup manufacturing did not need the seeds, many canners processed and sold their own seeds, providing major competition for tomato seedsmen. While the Livingston Seed Company managed to survive by selling other seeds, it dropped tomato seeds in the late 1930s.

During the 1930s the company moved into field seeds, such as alfalfa and sweet clover. Their last wholesale seed catalogue was published in 1947. Alan Livingston, the great-grandson of Alexander Livingston and grandson of Robert Livingston, sold the company in 1979 to Forest Randolph, who operated it under the name of Livingston, Ltd. The company was later acquired by Robert Johnston, who continues to operate it under the name of the Livingston Seed Company, Inc. Of course, Johnston sells tomato seeds, although mainly to retailers and home gardeners.[38]

Of all of Alexander Livingston's tomato varieties, only the Golden Queen and the Stone have been continuously available on the market since their introductions. Until recently, only a few of Livingston's other varieties were thought to have survived. However, searches of the USDA's list of tomato accessions have found several varieties thought extinct, some of which are for sale by seedsmen. Jeff McCormack at Southern Exposure Seed Exchange, for instance, has carried the Stone, Paragon, Beauty, and Favorite. Totally Tomatoes sells Livingston's Paragon. The Tomato Growers Supply Company sells Livingston's Paragon and has carried Golden Queen. Others are available through Seed Savers Exchange, including Livingston's Perfection.[39]

The Reynoldsburg Tomato Festival

In celebration of Livingston and others who have grown and enjoyed tomatoes, Reynoldsburg hosts a tomato festival. It began in 1965, when the Franklin County

Historical Society dedicated a plaque at the municipal building identifying Reynoldsburg as the "Birthplace of the Tomato." In the same year, the Ohio legislature adopted tomato juice as the official state beverage. To commemorate Reynoldsburg's tomato-rich past, the community decided to host a festival. The annual Reynoldsburg Tomato Festival has been held every year since, beginning on the Wednesday after Labor Day and ending the following Sunday with an impressive parade through town.

The festival involves much of the surrounding community, with businesses and individuals organizing all manner of events, exhibit tents, and booths, from which assorted tomato products and ephemera are shown and sold. One of the festival's organizers, Alcy Haden, has collected more than three hundred pieces of tomato paraphernalia, ranging from tea kettles and umbrellas to a tomato flag designed and sewn especially for her. Prize-winning recipes have ranged from tomato soup spice cake to tomato butter to ketchup caramels, and many of these dishes are available for consumption at the fairgrounds. To date, the festival record for largest tomato is 4½ pounds, and for tallest plant, 17 feet 5½ inches.

By unofficial count, the festival draws more than 35,000 tomato lovers from around the world, making it the largest celebration of the tomato, and ensuring that the spirit of Alexander Livingston, his sons, and grandsons lives on.

ANDREW F. SMITH

NOTES

1. Andrew F. Smith, "The Early History of the Tomato in South Carolina," *Carologue* 11 (Summer 1995): 8–11; Charles Sumner Plumb, "Seth Adams: A Pioneer Ohio Shepherd," *Ohio Archaeological and Historical Quarterly* 43 (January 1934): 14–15.

2. Letter from Thomas Ewing to the Athens County Pioneer Association, July 3, 1871, in "The Autobiography of Thomas Ewing," edited by Clement C. Martzolff, *Ohio Archaeological and Historical Quarterly* 22 (January 1913): 187.

3. *Western Reserve Magazine* 1 (July 1845): 100; *Country Gentleman* 38 (December 25, 1873): 820; Bertha E. Josephson, ed., "Ohio Recipe Book of the 1820s," *Mississippi Valley Historical Review* 36 (June 1949): 103, 107; *Western Tiller* 2 (August 21, 1829): 395; *Farmer's Reporter* 1 (June 1831): 38; Fanny Trollope, *Domestic Manners of the Americans* (New York: Reprinted for the bookseller, 1832), 61.

4. Martin Welker, *Farm Life in Central Ohio* (Cleveland, Ohio: Western Reserve Historical Society Tract No. 86, 1895), 4:55; *Livingston and the Tomato*, 19.

5. *American Farmer* 4 (May 1822): 40; *Germantown Telegraph*, November 3, 1847; *Country Gentleman* 19 (May 15, 1862): 318; *Genesee Farmer* 1 (September 10, 1831): 293; *Historical Magazine* 6 (January 1862): 35–36; *New England Cultivator* 1 (September 1852): 258; *Lancaster Farmer* 2 (March 1870): 52; *Genesee Farmer* 5 (March 7, 1835): 78; *Horticulturist* 4 (September 1849): 422; *Boston Courier*, August 1, 1845.

6. Cincinnati *Farmer and Mechanic* 2 (July 30, 1834):143.

7. *Ohio Farmer and Western Horticulturist* 2 (August 1, 1835): 119; *Cincinnati Daily Gazette*, August 18, 1835; *Daily Cleveland Herald*, August 22, 1835; *Ohio State Journal and Columbus Gazette*, September 4, 1835; *Botanico-Medical Recorder* 6 (November 4, 1837): 39–40; *Botanico-Medical Recorder* 6 (November 18, 1837): 58–59; *Botanico-Medical Recorder* 6 (January 27, 1838): 136–37; *Botanico-Medical Recorder* 6 (March 10, 1838): 186; *Botanico-Medical Recorder* 6 (April 7, 1838): 217–18; *Botanico-Medical Recorder* 6 (August 11,

1838): 358–60. For more information about Bennett and his tomato campaign, see Andrew F. Smith, *The Saintly Scoundrel: The Life and Times of Dr. John Cook Bennett* (Urbana: University of Illinois Press, 1997), 34–41.

8. *Hartford Daily Courant,* September 18, 1839.

9. *Philanthropist,* July 14, 1837–March 10, 1840; *Advertiser and Journal,* May 22–June 27, 1839; *Circulating Business Directory* (Philadelphia: Morris's Xylographic Press, 1838), 97; *U.S. Gazette,* August 25, 1838; *Philanthropist,* January 2, 1838; *Philadelphia Botanic Sentinel* 4 (March 15, 1838): 235; *Western (Cincinnati) Christian Advocate* 4 (September 8, 1837): 78; *Southern Agriculturist* 10 (November 1837): 615; *Catholic Telegraph,* as quoted in the *Hartford Daily Courant,* September 10, 1839; *Cincinnati Journal and Western Luminary,* October 3, 1837; *Troy Times,* October 10, 1838; *Louisville Daily Herald* and *Jeffersonville Courier,* as quoted in the *Connecticut Courant,* June 15, 1839.

10. *New York Times and Commercial Intelligencer,* July 19, 1839; *Western Sun and General Advertiser,* April 27, 1839–January 4, 1840; *United States Gazette,* August 25, 1838; *Philanthropist,* October 2, 1838; *New York Sun,* September 20, 1839; *Connecticut Courant,* November 30, 1839; *New York Express,* July 15, 1839; Robert Buist, *The Family Kitchen Gardener* (New York: J. C. Riker, 1847), 126; *Cincinnati Daily Gazette,* August 17, 1840. For more about tomato pills, see Andrew F. Smith, *The Tomato in America: Early History, Culture and Cookery* (Columbia: University of South Carolina Press, 1994), 102–31.

11. *Western Farmer and Gardener* 1 (November 1839): 69–70; Edward James Hooper, *The Practical Farmer, Gardener and Housewife* (Cincinnati, Ohio: Geo. Conclin, 1842), 493–96; Lettice Bryan, *The Kentucky Housewife* (Cincinnati: Shepard & Stearns, 1841), 22–25, 168, 171–72, 174, 183, 216, 217, 218, 366, 366–67; G. Girardey, *Höchst nützliches Handbuch über Kochkunst* (Cincinnati: F. U. James, 1842), 5, 6, 112; George Girardey, *Manual of Domestic Economy* (Dayton, Ohio: John Wilson, 1841), 8, 26, 80.

12. Edward Hooper, *The Practical Farmer, Gardener and Housewife* (Cincinnati: Geo. Conclin, 1842), 493–94.

13. *The Volunteer's Cook-book: For the Camp and March* (Columbus, Ohio: Joseph H. Riley and Company, 1861), 31; Robert Leslie Jones, *History of Agriculture in Ohio to 1880* (Kent, Ohio: Kent State University Press, 1983), 223–24.

14. *American Agriculturist* 7 (May 1848): 137–38; *Genesee Farmer* 1 (July 1831): 233.

15. *Genesee Farmer* 17 (May 1856): 156.

16. *U.S. Gazette*, as in the *American Farmer*, 2d ser., 3 (October 1841): 181; Charles Wilkes, *Narrative of the U.S. Exploring Expedition*, 5 vols. (London: Wiley and Putnam, 1845), 3: 309, 335; Nelson Klose, *America's Crop Heritage: The History of Foreign Plant Introduction by the Federal Government* (Ames: Iowa State College Press, 1950), 29.

17. *Horticulturist* 10 (March 1, 1855): 130–34.

18. Fearing Burr, *The Field and Garden Vegetables of America* (Boston: Crosby and Nichols, 1863), 643–54; Fearing Burr, *The Field and Garden Vegetables of America* (Boston: J. E. Tilton, 1865), 628–42.

19. *American Gardening* 16 (June 5, 1895): 214–15.

20. Burnet Landreth, "History of the Tomato," *Meehan's Monthly* 6 (March 1896): 39.

21. *Genesee Farmer* 17 (May 1856): 156; Liberty Hyde Bailey, *The Survival of the Unlike* (New York: Macmillan, 1897), 481; U. P. Hedrick, ed., *Sturtevant's Edible Plants of the World* (New York: Dover, 1972), 460.

22. Cornelia Parkinson, *Alex Livingston: The Tomato Man 1821–1898* (Reynoldsburg, Ohio: Published by the author, 1985), 4, 7; Cornelia Parkinson's notes on a presentation by Alan Livingston at the May 1995 meeting of the Livingston House Society, 2–3; interview with Alan Livingston, January 26, 1998.

23. *Livingston and the Tomato*, 20–21.

24. *Livingston and the Tomato*, 23–24.

25. *Gardener's Monthly* 25 (October 1883): 301; *American Agriculturist* 41 (March 1882): 126; Landreth Seed Company, *Descriptive Catalogue of the Garden, Seeds Cultivated on the Grounds of David Landreth* (Philadelphia, 1887), 57.

26. Liberty Hyde Bailey, "The Origin of the Tomato; from a

Morphological Standpoint," *American Garden and Floral Cabinet* 8 (April 1887): 22.

    27. Landreth Seed Company, *Descriptive Catalogue of the Garden, Seeds Cultivated on the Grounds of David Landreth* (Philadelphia, 1887), 57.

    28. Robert Buist, *Buist's Garden Guide and Almanac* (Philadelphia, 1890), 101–3; Liberty Hyde Bailey, "The Origin of the Tomato; from a Morphological Standpoint," *American Garden and Floral Cabinet* 8 (April 1887): 23.

    29. *Gardener's Monthly* 25 (July 1883): 205, 368; *Gardener's Monthly* 25 (March 1883): 82.

    30. *New York Tribune,* as quoted in the *American Farmer,* 9th ser., 3 (May 1, 1884): 135.

    31. A. W. Livingston's Sons, *Livingston's Seed Annual* (Columbus, Ohio, 1887), 44–45; A. W. Livingston's Sons, *Livingston's Seed Annual* (Columbus, Ohio: 1890), 11.

    32. Landreth Seed Company, *Descriptive Catalogue of the Garden, Seeds Cultivated on the Grounds of David Landreth* (Philadelphia: 1897), 50; *Garden and Forest* 5 (October 12, 1892): 488.

    33. A. W. Livingston's Sons, *Livingston's Seed Annual* (Columbus, Ohio: 1887), 44–45.

    34. *Livingston and the Tomato,* 37.

    35. A. I. Root, J. W. Day, and D. Cummins, *Tomato Culture* (Medina, Ohio: A. I. Root Company, 1892); A. I. Root Company, *Catalog of Seeds for the Greenhouse, Garden and Farmer, 1886–1895,* 18th ed. (Medina, Ohio, 1895), 3–4.

    36. *Rural New Yorker* and the *Elmer Times,* as quoted in the Livingston Seed Company, *Catalogue for 1899* (Columbus, Ohio, 1899): 5.

    37. *Yearbook of Agriculture 1937* (Washington, D.C.: Government Printing Office, 1937), 123; Victor Boswell, "Improvement and Genetics of Tomatoes, Peppers, and Eggplant," *Yearbook of Agriculture 1937* (Washington, D.C.: Government Printing Office, 1937), 179–81.

    38. Interview with Alan Livingston, January 26, 1998.

    39. Craig LeHoullier and Carolyn Male, *Off the Vine* 1 (February 1995): 12–13.

ACKNOWLEDGMENTS

M ANY PEOPLE HAVE assisted in preparing this facsimile edition of *Livingston and the Tomato*. By far the most significant was James R. Huber, resident of Truro Township, Franklin County, Ohio, who escorted me around Reynoldsburg, gave me a tour of the Livingston House, arranged for my participation in the 1996 Reynoldsburg Tomato Festival, offered his Livingston catalogue and ephemera collection for use, corrected the errors in the introduction, and constantly urged the process forward. I would also like to thank Alan W. Livingston, great-grandson of Alexander W. Livingston, who consented to interviews and offered valuable information about the Livingston family and its seed business. Needless to say, any errors remaining in the work are my sole responsibility. Thanks also to Keith Crotz of the American Botanist, Chilicothe, Illinois, who encouraged the project from its inception, and to Cornelia M. Parkinson, president of the Reynoldsburg-Truro Historical Society, for her assistance with information about Alexander Livingston's life.

A.F.S.

LIVINGSTON

AND THE

TOMATO

Yours Truly

A. W. Livingston

LIVINGSTON

AND THE

TOMATO.

BEING THE HISTORY OF EXPERIENCES IN DISCOVERING
THE CHOICE VARIETIES INTRODUCED BY HIM,

WITH

PRACTICAL INSTRUCTIONS FOR GROWERS.

BY

A. W. LIVINGSTON.

PUELISHED BY
A. W. LIVINGSTON'S SONS, SEEDMEN,
COLUMBUS, OHIO.

INDEX.

NOTE.—See Alphabetical Index at the end of the book.

BIOGRAPHICAL SKETCH.

M R. A. W. LIVINGSTON belongs to that honorable race of people known in America as the Scotch-Irish. His parents came from Cambridge, New York, to Reynoldsburg, Franklin County, Ohio,—ten miles east of Columbus, the capital city. The country was a wild wilderness of primeval forests at that time—1815; and required the labor of a generation or two of hardy pioneers to clear away.

He was born in 1822, and reared to a life of pioneer farming. School privileges were very limited then, but he learned to spell, read and write well, to "cipher in arithmetic as far as the Rule of Three;" and he often relates how he was privileged to study grammar for half a day.

At seventeen years of age his mother died, leaving him at a time when early manhood rejoices in the needed sympathies which a mother can best extend. The good Book explains it, "as one whom his mother comforteth."

When twenty-one years old he went to work for a gardener of the place. He hired to work four months, at eight dollars per month, only a little over thirty cents a day. Here he received and noted valuable items of information which his ready mind quickly grasped, and made the basis of calculations for the future. Indeed, it is one of the most striking characteristics of his mind that he was a close observer of all things that passed before his eyes. Everything different from what he had before seen was always noted; and it was followed up to the last change that might possibly occur to it, so painstaking was he to be accurate in these things. If a bird flew over his head having a new color or note of song he observed it, and watched it ever after to learn all that could be known of its habits. If a worm crawled beneath his feet he did not despise it; but noted all its goings and doings, and often became, for wise ends, the defender of those which all sought to kill. Insects, too, claimed his attention. If the Katydid sang in the same bush every evening for several months, he did not accept the statements of the learned who say (as in Webster's Unabridged Dictionary, The American Encyclopedia, and in Natural Histories) that it is the well-known large green grasshopper. It makes only similar noises to other grasshoppers, and it hops here and everywhere, never returning to the same place again at nightfall; while the Katydid is never seen but is always heard, there in the same bush or tree, from night to night, with her unchanging note, " Ka-ty-did " and " Ka-ty-did-n't." He takes nothing second-handed which he can prove for himself; and these tests he prosecutes with willfully persevering patience and zest. His interest was always keen in all kinds of plants and weeds. He was at an early age recognized among neighbors and friends as authority on them, because of the closeness and accuracy of his observations. Being of such a turn, and when he reached his majority working for a gardener and seed-grower, no doubt made a deep impression upon his active mind and gave it an early bias and taste for that kind of business. He did not then think of becoming a seed-grower himself.

For some months longer he worked by the day at chopping, ditching, general farming, or anything that came to hand, never receiving above fifty cents a day for his work, but never lying idle. Truly times have changed for the better, though some discontented people are saying, " Oh, what hard times these are ! " By this time he had grown to be a large, strong man physically, having excellent health. He had also a sunny, genererous, sanguine disposition.

At twenty-three years of age he married Miss Matilda Graham, a farmer's daughter, not blessed with more of this world's goods than himself, but rich in health, womanly grace, and that sound good sense which made her an helpmeet indeed. This union was blessed in due time by ten children—seven sons and three daughters—the oldest dying in infancy and the rest still living, and most of them engaged in some department of the seed trade.

Mr. Livingston, about a year later, leased a farm of one hundred and thirteen acres for one hundred and fifty dollars per year. He engaged in farming, trading in stock, growing seed for the trade, and making experiments with vegetables in order to test his ideas about them ; these were of great value in later

years. This consumed eleven years of his life, but the
range of experience through which he passed during
that time let him learn the ways of the world, and aided
him to master the business which was soon to claim his
closest attention. By this time he had accumulated
enough to purchase a farm of fifty acres; and about the
same time the seed-grower and dealer for whom he had
formerly labored concluded to move to Iowa. He
bought from him four hundred boxes of garden seeds,
then out on commission. He quit farming altogether
and embarked in the garden seed business exclusively.
For twenty years this commission business steadily increased, until in 1877 he had four thousand four hundred
boxes out in Ohio and the several surrounding States.

During these long years he continued his studies in
the processes of nature, and kept on with careful experiments to secure new and improved vegetables, such as
the trade demanded. He visited many state and county
fairs, learning what he could, and spent hundreds of
dollars to get personally acquainted with growers, and
to know the special needs of market gardeners in all
parts of the country. Whenever he introduced anything new and gave it his endorsement as a good thing,
the leading seedsmen of the country gladly catalogued
them, and do so still. One of them bought enough of
trial packets, of twenty-five seeds each, to raise five
hundred pounds of seed from them the first year, *without having seen them, but solely upon Mr. Livingston's reputation.* Such substantial endorsement of his integrity
and ability has always been received with gratitude
toward his competitors in the same line of trade.

Owing to the severe losses of '76 and '77, well re-membered by seedsmen selling on commission through the merchants of the country, Mr. Livingston concluded to quit the commission business altogether, and sell direct to growers. He therefore moved to Columbus, O., and there made arrangements to carry out those plans, because he could from this point reach two-thirds of the United States in twenty-four hours. His motto from the first was, " Give every man the worth of his money," with the idea that he would be thus (on merit) secured as a permanent customer. Subsequent events have shown this to have been a wise move for all concerned. He also grew specialties on contract for other prominent seedsmen, who appreciated new vegetables of un-doubted merit, and whose customers were willing to pay well for them with their endorsement.

After a few years of this work, his sons having en-tire charge of the business in Ohio, he set his eye upon the virgin soils of Iowa, with a view of enlarging this department of the seed business there. He moved in 1880 to the growing city of Des Moines, Iowa. Here he tested the suitability of the soil and location for seed growing, and found it to be most excellent for many kinds, and then hoped, with the consent of the firm, A. W. Livingston's Sons of Columbus, O., to have all moved in time to the new and thrifty West.

However, under the safe and upright management of his son Robert, the business in Ohio grew so rapidly and became so remunerative, that all thought of remov-ing it West was abandoned by the above firm. But being in Iowa himself, and several sons with him, and the soil so rich and easy to work, Mr. Livingston considered it wise to remain there, and with them engage in seed raising, which he did for nearly ten years. He finally aided and encouraged a younger son, Josiah Livingston, to commence in the seed business there in Iowa's capital city.

Most of the time since he quit the commission business has been spent in experimenting with new varieties, and introducing them to the public as soon as found fixed in type and habit of growth; and also having sufficient distinctness to entitle them to a new place and a new name. The account of his experiences in the Tomato line will be found in greater detail in the early paragraphs of this volume. The whole responsibility of the business has now for some years been in the hands of his sons and their growers. By this means, and since the departure of his wife a few years ago, Mr. Livingston was given what he had always desired, *opportunity to travel everywhere, sell seeds, and learn more about the business in his own matchless way—especially what was needed for market-gardeners.* The reader cannot fail to see that, by nature, by experience, and by application, Mr. Livingston is fully qualified to do what he tells us he has done in the body of this book; and that we have reason to expect that his hints, directions, and advices on Tomato Culture will be both practical and lucretive.

Although he was so busy all his life with the work of his choice, he found time to be one of the foremost men of his community in all matters of public interest.

In hospitality, needed improvements, larger educational facilities, and disinterested liberality, he never took a second place. In the advanced reforms of his times, and in the political concerns of his country, he kept himself well-informed to date. He was no mean antagonist to meet in a hand to hand argument on the living questions of the day. He was not afraid to take advanced grounds on all important matters, but he was so good-natured himself, so fair in his treatment of those who radically differed from him, that only in a few instances did any one ever get angry at him because of his utterances. He aimed to make what he said consistent with what he did.

From early life he was connected in full membership with the United Presbyterian Church, and has been an honored officer in it almost ever since. Never is there a meeting of any kind in his home congregation, which is not blessed with his presence, counsels, and prayers. He is a man of large sympathies and vast experiences. Little children run to meet him, young people confide to him their secrets, all love to see him coming, for they will learn something useful in life, and nothing done for his comfort will escape his notice or evade his high appreciation.

INTRODUCTION.

IT has not been my purpose to write an exhaustive
work on this increasingly popular fruit and vegetable.
My aim has been to aid the seedsmen, growers, and canners, to know what time, labor, close application, and
experience in the field have revealed to me that is practical and for their advantage in Tomato culture. Many
things will not be new to the experienced grower, and
ought not to be ; but some things will be novel and useful to many of my readers.

I express my indebtedness to my fellow-seedsmen,
with many of whom, in different parts of the country, I
have exchanged ideas and experiences *about the Tomato*,
with all freedom. While we do not endorse all the conclusions to which experimenters come, and publish in
their Bulletins, yet we strongly endorse the work in
which they are engaged, and acknowledge many useful
suggestions from them, to some of which we give place
here. It would be vastly better for growers if they
were, for all kinds of crops, to take advantage of these
public aids provided for their special benefit by the
States in which they live. Many good points I have
had first suggested to my mind by the frankness with

which our customers relate their experiences with their crops. Especially do I acknowledge the aid from growers whose ideas and conclusions I have included here with my own, in order to get to my attentive reader the greatest amount of knowledge in the most readable shape.

Trusting that whoever is influenced by these pages may reap as the fruits of his labor an abundant harvest, I submit this little book to the thoughtful consideration of my readers.

THE AUTHOR.

Columbus, Ohio.

Livingston and the Tomatoes.

1. The First Tomato I Ever Saw.—Well do I remember the first tomato I ever saw. I was ten years old, and was running down one of those old-fashioned lanes, on either side of which was the high rail fence, then so familiar to all Ohio people. Its rosy cheeks lighted up one of these fence-corners, and arrested my youthful attention.

I quickly gathered a few of them in my hands, and took them to my mother to ask, " What they were?" As soon as she saw me with them, she cried out, " You must not eat them, my child. They must be poison, for even the hogs will not eat them."

"But what are they, mother?" I asked.

"Some call them 'Jerusalem Apples;' others say they are 'Love Apples;' but, now mind, you are not to eat them. You may go and put them on the mantel, they are only fit to be seen for their beauty."

This I did, adding purple and yellow ones to this red one, and soon had quite a collection on display. The wild tomatoes bore small, hollow, tough, sour, watery fruit. They were no more like the new and improved varieties of to-day than the Pennyroyal cattle then, were like the Shorthorns now seen in our pastures everywhere.

From that early date the tomato became an object of special interest to me. Little did I then think, or for many years afterwards, that it was destined to make my name famous among seedsmen, market gardeners, canners, and horticulturists the world over. Nor could I any better foresee that it would furnish myself, my children, and my children's children, the necessaries and many of the comforts of life.

Thus it ever is: Dame Nature richly rewards those who keep close to her methods of operation, and who are not ashamed to remain tied to her apron-strings.

As the years passed by reckless people began to eat them, and as it became generally known that they were not poisonous, they came into more general use. New and slightly improved kinds were soon put on the market; but all efforts in this line for years did not get anything other than rough, imperfect fruits.

2. My Aim.—Years had come and gone with me, as the reader will see by reference to the sketch of my life in the opening of this book. My aim from the first was to grow tomatoes smooth in contour, uniform in size, and better flavored. Here my habits of close observation upon the processes of nature in all matters of reproduction stood me in good hand, but were not equal to the task by the method which I tried at first. For I tried the best kinds then known to the public, and se-

lected from these such SPECIMEN TOMATOES as approached
in qualities what was needed, or was in demand. The
seed from these were carefully saved, and when planted
were given the best cultivation possible, hoping in this
way to attain what I desired. After fifteen years of
the most scrupulous care and labor of this kind, I was
no nearer the goal than when I started in the race. According to laws of life, now well known, but which I did
not then understand, such stock-seed would reproduce
every trace of their ancestry, viz., thin-fleshed, rough,
and undesirable fruits. I ran this method through all
its changes, for the demand was constantly increasing,
and I desired to get a distinct variety that would have
good qualities and produce after its kind. Like many
others who were striving for the same thing, I wanted
it very badly.

Some improvements, however, were attained, but
mostly by improved conditions only, and as soon as
gained in the least degree, they were put upon the market under various names; such were the Fejee, the
Perfected, the Conqueror, the Canada Victor, the Tilden,
the Trophy, and others. With these, with my own, and
with any others I could get hold of that promised me
any gain, I tried again and again by varied selections of
specimens and good cultivation, to attain the desired
end. But I failed altogether. After such long and re-
peated failures it was with little hope that I turned to
other methods. I did not like to give up, "whipped out
entirely," in any matter I had set my mind and heart
upon, as I had in this thing; and I reasoned that I might

better be trying whatever came to hand to do, than to
do nothing.   So I kept a watchful eye upon my fields
for any *"leadings"* that promised to afford me the
smooth, well-flavored fruit, as we see it now in all the
markets of the world.

3. My New Method.—Whether this method I
here describe was new to others at that time (in the
Sixties) I did not know, but it was altogether new to
me; in fact it was a pure discovery on my part.   Let my
readers note that an ounce of experience is worth a ton
of theorizing.   I am giving actual experiences.   The
learned or unlearned may alike think as they will, but I
know I got what no living man had before.   There was
not in the United States at that time an acre of tomatoes from which a bushel of uniformly smooth tomatoes
could be gathered, as they are now grown everywhere.
I know, also, that I secured this result by the method I
hereafter describe.   I know, too, that I can repeat the
process at will, securing new varieties which will again
produce after their kind; and, at least, under my cultivation, will never deteriorate, or *"run out."*   For they are
ORIGINAL, DISTINCT VARIETIES, and will bring forth their
like, as will anything else; and they are as capable of
being cultivated into "strains" as are those of cattle,
hogs, chickens, or other plants and fruits of distinct kinds.
The same laws of life and breeding govern tomatoes
as in any other form of life, for all the processes of
nature are so simple that few will believe them, even
when they are pointed out to them.   With these pre-
liminary remarks I describe my new method.

In passing over my fields of growing tomatoes, which were still of all sizes, sorts and shapes, my attention was attracted to a TOMATO PLANT having distinct characteristics, and bearing heavy foliage. It was unlike any other in the field, or that I had ever seen. It showed itself very prolific, its fruit was uniformly smooth, but too small to be of general market value. As I examined it closely, observing how alike every tomato was on the stalk, wishing they were larger, and meditated over its possibilities long, it came to me like an inspiration, "WHY NOT SELECT SPECIAL TOMATO PLANTS instead of SPECIMEN TOMATOES." At any rate, I acted at once on this idea. The seeds from this plant were saved with pains-taking care, and made the basis of future experiments. The next spring, from these seeds, I set two rows across my garden—about forty rods long each —and to my glad surprise they all bore perfect tomatoes like the parent vine. I felt that

> My battle was half won,
> My race, too, half run.

They were a little larger, for which I also rejoiced, as I hoped to bring them up by choice cultivation to what would now be considered a medium-sized tomato, which I then thought, and still think, to be the most profitable size. The seeds from this crop were again carefully harvested, but from the first ripe and best specimens I selected stock for my own planting. By good cultivation and wise selection from season to season, not to exceed five years, it took on flesh, size, and improved

qualities. I then put it on the general market. This
was in 1870. Although grown and sold extensively all
these years to date, and although cultivated into various
"strains" by different growers according to their particular fancies, it is to-day the same distinct variety which
it was at the first. On account of its superior excellence
in comparison with all others in the market at that
time, I called it "THE PARAGON TOMATO."

PARAGON TOMATO.

4. Livingston's Paragon Tomato.—It was the
first perfectly and uniformly smooth tomato ever introduced to the American public, or, so far as I have
ever learned, the first introduced to the world. In color
it is a blood red. It has a strong, vigorous stalk; heavy
foliage; is a very hardy plant; will bear shipping of its
plants well; grows shoots or branches near the roots

later in the season, which bring a late crop equal in
size, quality, and evenness of ripening, to that grown
earlier on the center stem; and with its heavy foliage it
endures early frosts longer, and still produces crops
when the price is usually good. It is very prolific, a
little late, but is a most popular tomato as the annual
sales of seeds still show. From the very first of its history to this day, where acres were planted not a rough
or inferior tomato could be found in the entire fields.

This discovery, like all others, soon produced a
revolution. As a general field-crop tomato culture had
been of little general interest up to this date. To be
sure, Mr. Harrison W. Crosby canned and sold the tomato as far back as the year 1848, but that which
caused it to increase phenomenally, and rival the potato
as a profitable crop to grow, was the discovery of the
Paragon, and the universally smooth varieties that followed it. With these, tomato culture began at once to
be one of the great enterprises of the country. Demands
of market gardeners soon called for other varieties,
which I supplied as they became clearly defined to me.

5. Livingston's Acme Tomato.—Several varieties of a purple color had gone upon our markets, such
as the Fejee and the Perfected, with some others. They
produced somewhat after their kinds, but always required a liberal " CULLING OUT " of inferior specimens.
Yet many market gardeners, especially in the Western
States, became partial to a purple-colored tomato ; and
this taste still prevails. As my Paragon was red, and

too late for early, and as I wished to try again the method by which I had discovered the Paragon, I set about
to secure an early purple tomato. I selected from a
field of growing tomatoes, as before, A PLANT which bore
small, uniform, early tomatoes, and which had its own
peculiarly marked characteristics; such as recommended
it to my judgment as being the tomato to meet the demands of the trade at that time. I saved the seeds

carefully, cultivated it up in a few years, and introduced
it in 1875 as a perfectly new and distinct variety, under
the name, "The Acme Tomato."

It is lighter in foliage than that of the Paragon,
and much earlier. In fact it is the earliest of the uniformly smooth varieties to the present time. A most careful experimenter says: "Last year the Acme was two
days later than the Mayflower, this year it is seven days

earlier. Last year Acme was seven days earlier than Paragon, this year thirty days earlier. Last year it ripened with the Trophy, while this year it was eleven days earlier than all others."

Other kinds will often have one or two " first early ripe " tomatoes on the stalk, while Acme will be earlier and have a far greater number of " first early " to the stalk than others. Mr. Wm. Meggat, the wholesale seed-grower, says, "In 1890 I tried Acme with 115 other varieties, and found the first ripe fruit on it." By special cultivation as described in Paragraphs 45, 49, it will show to still better advantage for earliness.

It is of a bright purple color, very tender, and fine fleshed. It is specially grown for home uses, but is also a good general-purpose tomato. Many prefer it above all others. In fertility, foliage, growth, earliness, smoothness, size and color, its distinct type is clearly all it was seventeen years ago. In 1890 I grew some plants to test this matter, from stock seed of 1880—ten years old; and the result showed them to be exactly what they had been ten years before, viz., distinct and true to kind. They are, as stockmen would say, "thorough-bred;" and, at least under our cultivation, show no disposition to "*run out.*"

6. Livingston's Perfection Tomato.—I found in my Paragon and Acme fields while growing, an occasional " sport " (as it were, one in a thousand), which was yet quite distinct from either of the above varieties. By experiment I found that these retained their peculiarities perfectly. The thought then occurred to me that I might secure improved kinds more easily and quickly than from fields of all sorts, as I had done in the other two already introduced. I was urged to secure a new tomato because a good shipper was in demand, for tomatoes were being shipped in large quantities from country towns and places into the large cities, and from

LIVINGSTON'S PERFECTION.

the far South into the North. At any rate I selected a plant from a field of Acme (a purple tomato) and secured what is known everywhere as Livington's Perfection Tomato—a blood red tomato—which I introduced in 1880. The stalk and foliage are lighter than those of the Paragon, but stronger than those of the Acme. The fruit is uniformly smooth like the others, only it is a little flatter from the stem to the blossom ends. Its blood red color is very desirable, meeting the fancies of the public, especially in the Eastern markets.   One particular advantage it has as a shipper, is that it begins to show ripening several days before it is fully ripe.   It also has a thick, tough skin, which is not easily broken in transit.   With this kind, inexperienced hands or pickers in the South, if directed to gather only those fully grown and showing a tinge of ripening, can be employed to gather the fruit; and the grower will not get it into the distant market green, wilted or spotted.   This is a good tomato for bulk of crop, almost anywhere and everywhere.

LIVINGSTON'S GOLDEN QUEEN.

7. Livingston's Golden Queen Tomato.—In one of the county fairs which I often attended for the purpose of selling seeds, I saw a very pretty yellow tomato.   As I was examining it closely, and admiring it, the owner saw fit to make me a present of one of them, which I prized highly, and took special care to preserve, test and improve.   I had it a number of years before I introduced it; but in 1882 I thought it advisable to give it a wider circulation, and so advertised it extensively under the above name. It is of a bright golden yellow color, uniformly smooth, good size, most prolific, early ripening, and is a first-class, all-purpose tomato. It is admitted to be the best flavored tomato in existence. It is often used by the busy housewife when she puts sliced tomatoes on her table to good advantage, by alternating layers of this yellow with red or purple varieties. It makes a dish, with proper seasoning, dainty and attractive enough for a king.

8. Livingston's Favorite Tomato.—By this time the fruit canning business had grown extensively, and tomatoes came in for a large share of this trade. I made it my business, as I traveled about the country, to learn the demands of these canning establishments, viz., what qualities in a tomato were peculiarly suited to their trade? Then, in order to meet the canners' desires, I selected from a field of Paragons a tomato quite distinct from it, as any one can see who grows them side by side in the field. This new tomato I improved, and introduced in 1883, naming it *Livingston's Favorite Tomato.*

It is an early, blood-red, smooth, and most prolific tomato. It has no open spaces about the seeds in cavity, or ridges and hollows from stem to blossom ends. It ripens evenly, is a solid, meaty tomato, and has thicker flesh parts, of finer fibre, than any other used up to that time. They are of fine, large size. One grower writes us from Wisconsin, "I grew them fourteen and a half inches in circumference." Another, from Maryland, says, "I put up 5,065 cases tomatoes off of eighteen acres of your Favorites." A large canner in Iowa told us, " I get one and a half to two cans per bushel more from Livingston's Favorites than from other tomatoes." He also

LIVINGSTON'S FAVORITE.

claimed that in a day's run of forty thousand cans this difference in favor of the Favorite made him over eight hundred extra cans above any other tomato he ever used. This one fact shows the importance of canners looking well after the kinds their growers raise for them.

9. Livingston's Beauty Tomato.—I discovered that nearly all market gardeners, at least west of Pennsylvania, were determined to have a purple-colored

tomato for their trade. I had also learned that new kinds
selected from the Paragon fields (a red-colored tomato)
possessed more vigor of stalk, and preserved well all the
other qualities so desirable in any tomato. I began to
watch for a new tomato, which would be the market
gardener's pride and profit.

Being a practical gardener of many years' experience myself, I had much advantage over those who were
only seedsmen, or mere experimenters, in knowing exactly what was needed to supply this demand; and I
was not slow to take this advantage for the good of all.
In due time, and by the same processes as in its pred-
ecessors, my labor was rewarded with what I claim to
be THE CROWN JEWEL OF THEM ALL. It has a stouter stalk
than the Acme; heavier foliage, that protects it from
the scalding hot sun; is slightly darker in its purple
color; almost, if not equally, as early, and much larger
than Acme, being deeper through from stem to blossom
ends. It is a constant bearer, "holding up" its size on
till the frosts kill the vines. It is particularly productive; when the fruit is left on a single vine to see how
many can be picked off ripe at one time, it is not un-
common to gather a peck at a single picking. Neither
has it a useless green, hard core in the center. What
is usually a hard, unripe center in others, is in this,
and in all my kinds, as good as any other part of
it for food. The seed cavities are small, and contain
few seeds; it ripens all over and through at the
same time, and is freest from skin cracks or "Black
Rot." It is a splendid shipper, and was + first

purple tomato that obtained extensive sales in the
Eastern markets. The attention of shippers in the
South is especially directed to this variety, because their
success depends on a kind that will "*hold up under*"
shipments for long distances. An extensive shipper

from Mississippi tells us, "I had 'Beauties' on open
freight for nine days, and they came out all right." It
was introduced in 1886, and it is now sold by all leading
seedsmen in the world more largely than any other. It
requires almost two and a half tons of seed from this
kind alone, to serve our own customers in their annual
demands, and other seedsmen also sell large quantities
of it.

10. Selling Under Seal.—I dislike very much to
say anything against others in the same line of trade
with myself; or anything that may even sound like it ;
for I claim to be one of the last men on earth who grows
"sore-headed" over the successes of my competitors. I
am also aware that if I do myself, and my tomatoes,
common justice in this book, that I lay myself liable to
be charged with an "*ad scheme;*" but as I write experiences here, it came to pass that, because of designing

persons unjustly seeking to enter upon other men's
labors, we were compelled to do as many other seedsmen did with other new vegetables, viz., "SELL UNDER
SEAL." This was a necessity to preserve our own reputation as upright seedsmen, and to keep the names which
we had wisely selected for each of our new tomatoes.
They were justly popular, but I found that they were
sold under various other names; that many were mixed

or crossed with other kinds, and so impure; I learned, also, that even our own kinds were sold under each other's names, or those of other well-known varieties; and thousands of dollars' worth of seed are still sold in the same way each year, although it is palpably dishonest by all those who do it knowingly. Beauty, and all purple tomatoes, are sold in Chicago for Acmes. About Detroit, Beauty tomatoes are sold under the local name "Fejee." In Florida it is sold for "Improved Acme." In Baltimore it is sold as "Prize-taker," while Paragon is sold as "The Queen" tomato. Each of the other kinds have met the same fate. We grow on our experimental garden many leading varieties other than our own, and by actual comparison are led to believe that because of similar characteristics, and also that introducers refuse to give an account of the origin of their new tomatoes, that many are simply the renaming of our popular kinds. Clearest proofs, multiplied, could be given of these, and similar things; and they *will* be given to anyone entitled to know them of us. But now we sell under Seal, ONLY OUR OWN VARIETIES, and these alone when grown near at hand, under our own supervision. When that stock is exhausted, we do not buy of other firms, but quit selling under seal.

11. Livingston's Potato-Leaf Tomato.—Many growers had heavy clay lands, and needed a tomato adapted to this kind of soil, and still prove a heavy cropper. The Potato-Leaf, which I introduced in 1887, was

found well calculated to meet this demand. I had it
ready before I got the Beauty, but considered it wiser to
let it wait until a *sweepstakes* tomato, like the Beauty,
was well under way. Its leaf resembles that of the Irish
potato, hence its name. It is like the Mikado or Turner's Hybrid, in *foliage* only; in every respect they differ
in their *fruits*. It is of fine flavor, uniformly smooth,

LIVINGSTON'S POTATO-LEAF.

deep through, good size, a bright, glossy, purple color,
an excellent producer, and is especially suited for "staking up," or "Trellising." See Paragraphs 45 and 49.

This Tomato, because of its right size and glossy
purple color is of all the purple varieties the best adapted
for canning whole, which is in the Eastern parts of the
country now becoming very common and popular.

12. Livingston's New Stone Tomato. — The American public is not satisfied with old things, however good they may be. I was asked almost every day, while "on the road," "Have you anything new in the tomato line?" Now, although customers had made it plain by thousands of unsought testimonials to those

LIVINGSTON'S NEW STONE.

already introduced, that there was very little opportunity left for improvement in tomatoes, I yet found it wise to put out new ones from time to time. Of course there was less difference between these and those I first introduced, than between my first and all kinds which preceded them. It was always my aim to please my

customers, and so I made these little improvements as
it became clearly necessary for the grower's profit. The
New Stone was found between rows of Beauty and Favorite, in the fields of one of our careful growers. It
was perfected as a distinct variety, and introduced in
1889. It is blood-red in color, shaped like the Beauty
—see Paragraph 9—and is the largest smooth red tomato on the markets. It is the heaviest for its size or
compass of all others; therefore its name, "Stone."
Some growers claim they can tell it from others of the
same size in the dark, because of its greater weight and
solidity. It comes more nearly combining the good
qualities of all the red tomatoes preceding it than any
others of any name. No red tomato carries its size
throughout the season better, none are more prolific,
none are better adapted for all purposes, none have
pleased our growers better in the same length of time
since its introduction. In my judgment the coming tomatoes that will hold the highest rank, and wear the
longest with those who grow them for the money they
will make them, are, for purple color, "THE BEAUTY;"
for red color, "THE NEW STONE."

13. Livingston's Royal Red Tomato.—It was
found among Dwarf Champion fields. These were purple tomatoes, while the Royal Red is a bright scarlet—
the reddest tomato through and through yet introduced
by us or others. I found that large quantities of tomatoes were used in the manufacture of catsup, and also
for canning whole in bottles. This very decided red

color was in demand for these purposes; so it was introduced as "Livingston's Royal Red," in 1891. It is a
first-rate general purpose tomato, however. It carries
in high degree most of the good qualities of the older

LIVINGSTON'S ROYAL RED.

ones I have introduced. In size, smoothness, productiveness, solidity, and beautiful appearance, it will please
the most fastidious. When on exhibition at our Fairs
it attracts more attention than any other of the red
varieties.

14. Livingston's Gold Ball Tomato.—The little
yellow Egg, or Plum Tomato, which people ate raw in
their gardens, and used so extensively for preserves,
suggested to my mind that a new and improved variety
for the same purposes might be very acceptable. One of

our best growers found it among his growing tomatoes, and it was introduced in 1892. It is a bright golden yellow, round as a ball, one and one-half inches in diameter; it has few seeds, abundance of flesh, and is so very productive that some single plants have borne a half bushel of fruit. The tomatoes will, without injury,

LIVINGSTON'S GOLD BALL.

hang on the vine in clusters a week or ten days after fully ripe. I consider this gem of a tomato the best I have ever seen for preserves. No thrifty housewife who once fixes her eyes upon this Ball of Beauty will ever let it go from her garden or table.

15. Livingston's Buckeye State Tomato.—
Lately considerable excitement among ambitious seedsmen has been experienced over very large fruited
tomatoes. Now this furnishes me with an opportunity

LIVINGSTON'S BUCKEYE STATE.

for which I have waited long. I have had this one,
named as above, from the very first of my all-smooth
varieties; I did not introduce it, because it seemed to
me too large for general use. It is the largest uniformly
smooth one in the markets that carries with it all the

qualities I have described as belonging to all others of
my great family of tomatoes.

As there is now a demand for large specimens, I
entrust mine to the judgment and experience of the
tomato growing public in the year 1893. There is
nothing coarse or rough about this fruit. It ripens quite
early, is a tomato for home use and for the home market;
a vigorous grower, has no green end or useless core, and
few seeds; is of fine flavor, purple color, and grows in
mammoth clusters of from six to ten in a cluster, many
of which will weigh from one to one and a half
pounds apiece. It is also a very profitable kind to stake
up or trellis. See Paragraphs 45 and 49.

**16. Livingston's New Dwarf Aristocrat To-
mato.**—It would seem after all that has been said of the
tomatoes already described, that no more could be added, or any other improvements made on them; yet there
are many more points of excellence to be attained, some
of which I claim are found in this new dwarf tomato
which will be introduced this year—1893. It has a
strong, erect, bushy stalk, that is often one and a half
inches in diameter. Because of its erect bearing and
dressy appearance it is called "The Aristocrat." The
plants are so stalky and stiff from the time they come
out of the ground that they reset without wilting or
falling down, and are therefore not stunted; nearly a
week on "*first early*" is gained in this way. Plants can
be set much closer than those of other varieties; at least
one-half more will be required to set the same plot of

ground. With this advantage, and their extra productiveness, I believe under special cultivation they will produce one-third more to the acre than other kinds. It begins to bear with the earliest varieties, and does not cease bearing until frosts kill the vines. Yet because of its erectness, bushy habits, and close standing in the field, it is saved from the early frosts, and only the hard freezes in the fall will reach the fruit hid up under its foliage, and thus bears abundantly when other kinds have been entirely killed. The fruit has the peculiar quality of keeping in a dry, cool room, before decay sets in, for three or four weeks after they cannot longer be trusted in the open field. It is also a large sized tomato, of a bright glossy red color, very fine fleshed and flavored, uniformly smooth, and is an all-purpose tomato for shippers, canners, market gardeners, and for fancy and remumerative home-culture. In a word, it carries the good qualities of its forerunners among my varieties, and has some others peculiar to itself. I prophesy a brilliant future for our Aristocrat.

17. Livingston's Large Rose Peach Tomato.— This sort originated with us and has all the general characteristics belonging to this singular and distinct class of tomatoes, but is much larger than any peach variety yet brought out, averaging about with the Acme in size. We have grown it for several years on our trial grounds here, and are well pleased with it. We pronounce it *rot proof* because we have not observed a single specimen showing any sign of rot in the past three years of

its growth. It is a profuse bearer until killed by re-
peated frost, and has the agreeable, mild flavor as well
as the suffused coloring and the peculiar peach-like
bloom on its surface. We presume that the texture of
the skin accounts for its never rotting, and we think for

LIVINGSTON'S LARGE ROSE PEACH.

the same reason it would be well adapted for growing
in certain hot climates where the ordinary tomato cannot be successfully grown. It is certainly worthy of
extended trial.

I HAVE now given the reader a history of the principal varieties already introduced. They were each secured to meet certain clearly defined demands arising in the tomato trade. If there is any demand which has not been reasonably met, I acknowledge frankly that I do not know what it is. Some will say, " This is a big-pictured advertisement." Now, I am free to admit that I am not blind to the fact that what I have related will advertise us among the readers of this book; but we will not allow that we are dealing with anything but the facts in the case. If facts advertise me, that is as legitimately mine as the tomatoes I have introduced ; and no one is injured if I claim my own. It can be no loss to the grower, nor to my fellow-seedsmen who catalogue my tomato seeds from year to year, and sell large quantities of them ; nor yet to the consumer who partakes of new and improved fruits. It will now be necessary to consider some of the questions relating to kinds, which many growers and others are continually asking, and which have been written about so variously, that " I, also, will show mine opinion."

18. " Will your varieties 'run out?'"—Under our cultivation, having our distinct kinds as a basis, there is no such thing as the degeneracy of the kinds. I have sweet corn kept pure and improving for forty-one years ; and cabbage so, for thirty-five years ; and tomatoes so, for twenty-six years. I see the same laws of life that govern pedigreed stock in animals, control in tomato life. If one has a distinct variety, and keeps it pure, and cultivated up, it cannot degenerate. All experience is against the idea of degeneracy; unless left to itself, to mix in foreign blood, to get under conditions unfavorable for its true and best developments. I am aware that it will not do to set out tomato plants that come up of themselves from the last year's crop, even when that crop was considered pure stock. It is left to itself, and whatever of bad nature there may be in it, is sure to come out. This I know to be a fact—volunteers will not do to use, although no one exactly knows why it is so. This does not argue, however, that a distinct kind, kept pure and cultivated under proper conditions, will degenerate; at least, mine do not " run out."

19. " Can we cross kinds and get new ones?"

That is, if I plant several kinds, such as Beauty, Mikado, and Dwarf Champion, together in the same field, so that they will mix in the bloom, can I get from a mongrel, thus produced, a new and distinct variety that will produce after its kind, and be better than either of the above varieties ? In answer to this question let me say, I have no confidence in hybridizing or crossing as a method of securing new varieties. I am not likely to forget my failures for fifteen years, nor the lessons which they taught me. Like begets like. Rough ones beget rough ones. From an imperfect kind uniformly perfect

specimens cannot come. " Blood will tell," and the imperfections will appear; and this will be true if there is
the least bad blood in either of the kinds that may be
crossed. If the Trophy is crossed with the Paragon the
result will be an improvement on Trophy, but rough
ones will still appear among them, and more "culls" will
appear. This fact can be easily proven in practice,
even where for several generations these bad qualities
had not been much seen, for some unaccountable reasons
they will begin to appear again. This is what is known
as " breeding back," among the stockmen, but is just as
true of tomatoes as of anything else. If any one breeds
crosses upon crosses, no one can tell what the result will
be. Yet trying to *breed in* certain good qualities by
crossing those that do not have them with some that do,
while at the same time certain bad qualities would be
bred out by the same process, must ever prove a failure,
simply because it violates the very constitution of things,
viz.: " Whose seed is in itself yielding fruit after
his kind." I see some seedsmen are advertising this
year, 1893, in their catalogues, the seeds of fifty different kinds of tomatoes in one packet. No one will get a
new and valuable kind from seed of such a mixed lot, for
they will not produce after the nice specimen tomatoes
one may select from them. It would be better to do as I
did—select A PLANT of decided markings of stalk, leaf, size,
quality of fruit to taste; for if you happened upon an
original variety it would then come true to kind; otherwise, never in the world; for it might in any season
" breed back " to the time when Jacob traded lentils to

Esau for his birthright. It is no manner of use wasting time on seed from crosses for stock seed. As well build a mill high on the hill and expect the water to run up there of its own accord to drive the machinery. It violates nature, and it can't be done that way. The whole trick in getting new varieties is in knowing which plants are original kinds, and those that will, under cultivation, take on size, flesh, and desired qualities, WITHOUT ANY INFUSION OF FOREIGN BLOOD. No doubt, on this subject, there is much of mystery as yet, just as there is on all subjects connected with life, which is itself a profound mystery. However, this makes it all the more inviting field for scrutinizing investigations.

20. Can distinct varieties be cultivated into different "strains?"—Each plant has its range of possibilities; that is, it can grow larger or smaller than a standard size, a little darker or lighter in color, a little more sour or sweet; and so on, covering all of its qualities. I suppose The Creator gave it these capacities to change in order to adapt itself to varying conditions under which it might have to grow, and still continue itself from year to year. Each plant has its limitations however, beyond which it cannot be cultivated. No amount of cultivation (or putting it under the most favorable circumstances to develop to its utmost) would grow a Yellow Egg Tomato into a Golden Queen, because "The Queen" has capacities beyond the limitations of "The Egg" tomato. Hence if we get Queen tomatoes we must not try to get them by cultivating up the Egg, but get a new and distinct variety.

There may be another reason why the Creator has arranged things in this way, viz.: it affords opportunity to gratify a great variety of tastes; suppose, as a gardener, I prefer " The Beauty " tomato to any other one kind. As I grow it from year to year, and observe it closely, I discover these variations in its qualities. I see some larger or smaller, some darker or lighter, some heavier or of less weight, and so on. At once my preferences would lead me to select for my stock-seed from specimen plants and tomatoes those which I thought best. Now, this process kept up for a number of years will produce what would be properly called my " Strain of Beauties." Yet let it not be forgotten, it would never become anything other than a Beauty.

Now, in point of fact, as I visit the fields of many careful tomato growers each year, the evidences of this very thing comes to my eyes. I will not be successfully contradicted when I say, there are to-day among gardeners, many strains of Paragon, of Beauty, and of other popular varieties. I sincerely hope, too, that the reader will not fail to consider that only distinct kinds are capable of being cultivated into decided " strains;" and this in turn, proves that my kinds are new and distinct.

For this reason, and because of many observations made in all parts of this country, I have great difficulty to see how any originator has got, even aproximately smooth tomatoes from rough kinds, without a strong infusion of blood. from some of my distinctly smooth varieties. In our trial gardens are raised many well-known principal kinds; and there are none of them but show a proportion of rough ones among them. There is, so far as I know, very little literature upon how originators secured the kinds they claim are new and distinct varieties, and which they introduce under various names. It would be of immense interest to me, and I judge to growers in general, to learn how they got them. I, for myself, would like to learn many things from these men if they are sending out those that are really new and distinct; but if they send out only "crosses," or "strains," as such, one would only smile at the effort, but expect no permanent results from it. I suspect, at least, that such efforts account for the prevailing opinion that the life of any distinct kind of tomato is only ten years.

21. Selected Stock - Seed. — We should have among seedsmen, for the benefit of growers, something which would procure the same end as the pedigrees of animals to be used for breeding purposes. Stock-seed should be selected, year by year, from the discovery of any new kind, so long as there is any demand for it, by the wisest and best growers in the land. All admit the necessity and advantages of such care, such cultivation, and such selections; but few go to the expense to do this. Concerning all the kinds introduced and before described, I can say they are really pedigreed tomatoes. From the day of their discovery to this day, they have been under our hands; so we know what we have, and what they will produce. Only a few men have been found who can be entrusted to save selected stock for us, and raise from it reliable seeds for our customers. These are well paid for this very responsible labor, and they can make a business of it, and so we keep our tomato seeds up to the standard type. All my varieties, nearly, are general and special purpose tomatoes. All are smooth—to a tomato—not a rough one can be found in acres, as we grow them. A son of Mr. Landreth, the seedsman, in the fall of 1892, at his own request, was taken over the fields of my different kinds in the trial gardens. After going through all the fields, he was challenged to say whether he had seen a single rough one among all of my own varieties, but he could not say that he had. The fact is, they are absolutely and uniformly smooth in contour. All ripen evenly, all over and through, at the same time. Not one has a useless core, or hard stem end; the whole tomato is all alike edible. All grow in clusters, and so are more prolific. All possess the greatest possible solidity in the smallest possible compass. And all are new and distinct varieties, producing after their kind.

While traveling, I am often asked to buy tomato seed. I could buy it by the hundred pounds at twelve cents to forty cents per pound. I know that large quantities of it are bought and sold in the seed markets to-day; because when sold at one dollar or more per pound, there may be a gain of three or four hundred per cent. But after what I have written, it is plain that no grower who would make the most of his opportunities should trust to that kind of seed. All my experiences and observations teach me to advise every grower always to get the best available selected stock-seed from reliable seedsmen. It is the cheapest in the end, by far. The importance—the money value—of having varieties true to kind, and good, strong seed from them, cannot be over-estimated. It often makes all the difference between what is loss, and what pays well, in one's crop. It costs more to get it, and we must always expect to pay more for it. After the first cost of the select stock-seed, it costs no more to raise and market the crop than it would if the market gardener grew it from inferior kinds. This latter seed would cost him at least one dollar per pound. An ounce will plant an acre. This amount would cost him six and a quarter cents per acre. If he will add six and a quarter cents more, he can get good seeds of profitable kinds. This would be at the rate of two dollars per pound. If he will add another six and a quarter cents, he can buy choice seed of better varieties; or at the rate of three dollars per pound. But if he will add yet another six and a quarter cents, he can have selected stock-seed from the first kinds in the land. This would be at the rate of four dollars per pound, or twenty-five cents per acre.

It is not always safe to get barely enough seed; for frost, accident, or other enemy, may destroy it. In the North growers usually buy and sow one-quarter pound for an acre, and twice that amount is used in the South. At the above figures the select stock-seed would cost per acre from one to two dollars. This amount is so small that no wise, wide-awake man will risk growing his crops from inferior kinds. The profits from the first picking off an acre will far more than pay this difference in the cost of seed; and the grower has, for all the rest of the season through, the choicest fruits to place before his customers. Who does not know among market gardeners, that you cannot sell a measure of mixed apples to advantage? Neither can you of tomatoes. Best kinds, in best condition, bring best prices, on all markets, from the best paying customers. After extended observations I am persuaded that there is more lost to the producers of all kinds of field crops by planting inferior seed than from any other one cause. People do not often think about it as it is. In one row of tomatoes forty rods long ONE INFERIOR STALK would, if it had been a good one, so increased the gain of the crop as to have bought select stock-seed for the whole row. This idea was given me by a sharp, shrewd, grower, who was making his business pay him richly. I am well aware that prices, as named above, will seem large to amateur growers; but experienced gardeners will take no exceptions to my reasoning here. It only costs a farmer or beginner a few cents to test the certainty of what I write here by his own experience.

22. Can farmers and market gardeners grow their own seed and save this expense?—I think not, because they plant to *use the fruit*, and not to *get the seed*. It is often to their advantage to plant different kinds side by side. They will cross badly, and so in a few years " *run out.*" " But could they not plant some separately and so get their own seed?" Yes, they could, if they would, and learn the seed-raising business; but will they do it? and would it pay them if they did? Seed-raising is another business altogether, which few market gardeners know anything about. The amount of seed—especially tomato seed—which any one uses is so small, that if he employed the time and labor necessary to save his own seed in producing marketable fruits, he could, by the gain from this, buy selected seed of the best kinds a half dozen times over. An old saying is, "Every man to his trade;" for those who make a business of any specialty can do that cheapest. So it comes to pass in human affairs that most of us find it pays best to do a few things well, and buy what we want cheaper, vastly cheaper, than we could if we tried to produce it for ourselves. Let us "live and let live." See what other writers think on this same subject:

SHOULD GARDENERS GROW THEIR OWN SEEDS.

BY W. J. GREEN.

"This question is usually answered in the affirmative: the reason assigned being that one can grow better seeds than he can buy. The reason may have been a valid one once, and may still hold good in some cases, but to advise private parties to grow their own garden seeds is about as antiquated advice as to recommend farmers to weave their own cloth.

"Indiscriminate advice is worse than no advice. This is one of the cases where careful discrimination is required. To grow good seed, it is not only necessary to keep varities pure, by preventing crossing, but it is also necessary to exercise the greatest care in selection of stock. It is not enough to secure a good variety and then keep it from mixing with other varieties, but trueness to type and purity of strain must be looked after. Imperfect forms must be weeded out, and only those that come up to the proper standard retained. The art of selection so as to obtain the best possible results is not so well understood as desirable, but professional seed growers know about all there is known about it. They could give private growers " pointers " every day in the year.

"There is no doubt but they know how to grow, and do grow, better seed than ninety-nine per cent. of private growers are able to do, and they sell their products at prices far below what small quantities can be grown for. The only possible good reason for any one to grow a small quantity of seeds for his own use is, that he thinks them to be much superior to anything that he can buy.

"In most cases such persons deceive themselves in the belief that they have something better than any one else is able to grow. But, says one, " If I have something that I know to be extra fine, will it not pay me to perpetuate it myself, so as to be sure of it?" The answer is, " yes, if you are sure that you can do the work better than any one else, but the chances are ten to one that a regular seed grower can do much better than you can, and do it vastly cheaper."

23. Hints to the American Seed Trade Association.

—There have been such mixing of varieties, and of names given to kinds by unscrupulous parties, that great and unnecessary expense has been occasioned. Possibly there has been not a little over-reaching in the race for wealth and distinction. Some course of action ought to be adopted, and lived up to, that would render this sort of thing practically impossible.

I recommend that the Association list all worthy vegetables under the name given it by the introducer, together with his description of the same, and that this be published in a book, called " Vegetable Standard," by the American Seed Trade Association. Also, that hereafter no vegetable shall be added to this list, as a new one, until the originator gives satisfactory proofs that it is a new kind, distinct from all those already listed, worthy a place in this Standard, and of the endorsement of the Association. The American Poultry Association does this with advantage to all. It is an acknowledged fact that deceptions are used in the seed trade; new names are assumed for old varieties by those without principle; they sell thousands of pounds of seed none should buy, and much less plant. Such need exposure before the public, for the benefit of all. I here add, as confirming what I have said, the words of a good writer from one of our Experimental Stations:

"In testing varieties at our station, we have forcibly noticed the confusion that exists in the names of vegetables, and have, many times, strongly felt the need of some authorized standard that would aid us in determining whether a given variety we are growing is distinct, or whether it is the same as some other, bearing a different name.

"Because we have discovered that there is no such standard, and because we are finding out that many of the names offered in our catalogues are not distinct, it has occurred to us that we can perhaps do no more useful work for horticulture than to make the effort to discover how many distinct varieties we have, and to make a complete and accurate description of each. It is certainly not our province to assign the blame for the confusion of names that exists. Indeed, the more we learn the more we become convinced that it is nobody's fault. It is the natural and inevitable consequence of carrying on the seed business without an authorized standard of varieties. It is what language was before we had a dictionary, and what our fruits would have been to-day, had not Mr. Downing and his associates accomplished the great work of sifting out the synonyms.

"The question has often been raised whether it is possible to make descriptions of varieties of vegetables which will apply to different soils and climates. Our botanist friends have often expressed grave doubts upon the subject, and have even declared it impossible. After three years of study in this directi_n, I am of the opinion that the thing is practicable, though it is certainly not easy of accomplishment."

Some kind of protection, too, ought to be found for

the right in these matters, and for those who walk up-
rightly. We cannot have it too soon, either. I have
thought that a national law to the effect that no one
should SELL THE SEEDS of any vegetable without consent
of the discoverer for five years from date of letters pat-
ent which the Government had given him for discovering a new and worthy vegetable was a just necessity.
If I had had such protection upon my new tomatoes,
there is not a seedsman in the land but knows it would
have been worth thousands of dollars to me, and would
not have been one dollar less advantage to the seed
trade of the country, or to those whom they serve. If
a man is entitled to seventeen years protection on any
new device of every sort, how much more ought the
seedsman or grower who discovers a new article of food
have protection for five years. I hope some member of
the Association, more familiar than I with the details of
this business, will work it out and put it through; for it
would give a wonderful impetus to the securing of new
and useful kinds of vegetables.

Here is another thing in which all seedsmen and
their customers are interested. There is an increasing
seed trade carried on by mail, and this is largely by the
poor of the land who only buy in small amounts. The
United States ought not to carry Canadian mail matter
at four cents per pound, and charge her own citizens
just double that rate, viz., eight cents a pound. I believe if the Association did but call the Government's
attention to it, this would be changed at once. England
is able to take care of herself, and this country ought to

give her own subjects (among which are seedsmen and growers) a better opportunity to be loyal and thrifty citizens by taking better care of themselves in a legitimate way.

24. Profits on a Tomato Crop.—I now propose to show that this is a profitable crop to raise. After all, if there is no demand for them, good kinds will help no one. If we cannot get a good price for them when they are grown, of what avail will improved varieties be to any one. This is shown in the history of the Golden Queen tomato. My readers have a right to know and be satisfied whether tomato growing is profitable or not. This point must be proven clearly, and I aim to do that here for any fair-minded person.

It is variously and correctly estimated that an acre will produce from one to eight hundred bushels of tomatoes. A man can grow as many acres of them, and be equally as certain of a good crop, as he could be of corn. Indeed, take the soils and seasons as they come and go, he would be rather more certain of a crop. He would now be quite as sure, also, of a ready market for the one as the other. Neither will it cost more labor, time, attention, or money, to produce tomatoes than to raise corn; and they have rather less enemies than any other field crop as extensively grown. Like other products of the soil, the price will vary according to the law of supply and demand. It will range from twenty-five cents to one dollar and a half per bushel. . Let us reason a little from these premises. If you harvest one hun-

dred bushels, and sell at twenty-five cents per bushel,
you get twenty-five dollars per acre. This is counted at
lowest acreage and lowest price per bushel. It will not
be better than that with corn, oats, wheat or hay, if you
count either of them at lowest acreage and lowest prices.
But, if you sell the one hundred bushels per acre at fifty
cents per bushel you will get fifty dollars; and if for one
dollar per bushel, one hundred dollars per acre.

Now, if you harvest four hundred bushels per acre
(one-half the largest possibility), and sell at twenty-five
cents per bushel, you get one hundred dollars; at fifty
cents per bushel, two hundred dollars; at one dollar per
bushel, four hundred dollars to the acre.

These results show up well when compared with
those of other crops which growers have been raising,
I venture to assert. Do you ask, "but are not these
imaginary figures?" I answer, "not a bit of it." This
very season—1892—tomatoes were readily sold on the
Columbus markets at from forty cents to one dollar and
a half per bushel; and we had in our own fields a good
many acres that did not fall short of the four hundred
bushels to the acre, either.

"But if all farmers went into the business of growing tomatoes, what then?" I am often asked such
questions. Every one will not do it; at least for many
years to come; and then, when it does not pay longer,
it will be time enough to change to some other crop.
The above question would apply equally well to any
other standard crop of the present time. It could be
asked with as much pith and point of the potato, corn,

or wheat crops. But there is no more danger of over-
stocking the markets with tomatoes than with any
other single crop that is commonly raised at this time.
To-day Ohio alone needs twenty-five more canning factories to be up with Iowa or Maryland. Southern shippers must make money, for there are thousands of them
in the business of raising tomatoes for the northern
markets. The selling prices range from two to eight
dollars per bushel, and they secure from fifty to two hundred bushels to the acre from the early spring crop, and
more per acre from the early summer crops. From the
above 'prices must be subtracted the commissions and
freights, but if that costs half its value, their returns will
still be from fifty to eight hundred dollars per acre. Information from the experimental stations shows that they
could be raised under glass or in hot-houses in the
North, and sold at spring or early summer prices with a
net profit of fifteen cents per square foot for the plat so
planted. There are nine square feet in a yard. This
would be a net profit of one dollar and thirty-five cents
to the square yard; or in a hot house one hundred feet
long, with beds a yard wide on each side of the walk, it
would bring two hundred and seventy dollars net gain.
And remember, this would come in after other good
paying crops had been taken off the same beds—such as
lettuce.

And if one grows the tomato for his own use, no
fruit, or other vegetable, will afford him such abundance
of healthful food for the same expenditure of labor.
This will enable my readers to see that there is money

in the business, with no more "drawbacks" than in any other line of products from the soil. Still, if a man has failed in all else, I could not advise him to try growing tomatoes for profit; but I will tell you that the kind of man who will, in my judgment, get the nearest to eight hundred bushels to the acre, and secure the nearest to one dollar per bushel for them. It will be the man who *aims* at these figures, leaving no stone unturned to get them, and working closer to it from year to year as *experience* teaches him what, and what not to do. He will dare to risk whatever reasonably promises to fetch better crops and better prices. The man who selects the best seeds, of the best kinds, for the best soil he has, works it most judiciously, uses wisely the right fertilizers, prepares it best for market, reads the best newspapers, is, with courtesy and honest dealing for all, the man who will succeed in growing good tomatoes and getting big money for them. Give this an all-around, faithful trial, and then write me a letter of thanks for calling your attention to it.

25. Selection of Kinds to Plant.—There are more than three hundred kinds of tomatoes; at least, there are above that number of names applied to them. It is charitable for me to say that each of these kinds have some qualities to recommend them. Many respectable fellow-seedsmen advertise some of these kinds, and all growers who have tried them, and find they pay them better than other kinds, would be very foolish indeed to abandon them. I do not wish to say anything

against any of these particular varieties, nor will I; but
the reader will easily believe, as I have discovered and
introduced thirteen different kinds, with a view of meeting the demands of the times, that I would at least prefer my own to all others. If I were to collate what the
Bulletins *decide*, and the money-making customers *say*,
of my tomatoes, in comparison with all other most popular varieties, I could not complain that my judgment
in this thing was not ably confirmed. I would gladly
avoid naming varieties suited to any given end the
grower might wish to attain; and yet, I hope my modesty will not be questioned when I say that I have every
reason to think that my readers will want to know
which of his kinds Livingston would plant for any given
purpose. I will name, then, only those heretofore described in this book.

26. Kinds for Shippers.—As these are earliest
on the market, I name them first. For early red, PER-
FECTION and THE ARISTOCRAT; especially in those parts
of the country where "*staking up*" is extensively employed. THE BEAUTY, of purple color, comes next, and
should be given place for one-half the whole crop. NEW
STONE for bulk of crop between early and late; this is a
red tomato, and very choice for this purpose. And PAR-
AGON for red late.

27. Kinds for Home Use.—I would name FA-
VORITE for early red, and ACME for early purple. BEAUTY
for bulk of crop. A few stalks of yellow GOLDEN QUEEN

is needed for slicing and preserves. For ornamental trellising and useful crop, try ROYAL RED, POTATO-LEAF, and yellow GOLD BALL. On fancy trellises they are very beautiful, and will repay the grower for his trouble in good fruits. If a farmer wishes large, fine-fleshed tomatoes, so that he can get a good price on market (should he have more than he wishes for himself), let him try BUCKEYE STATE, which is of purple color, and quite sweet in flavor.

28. Kinds for Market Gardeners.—ACME for first early purple, and PERFECTION for first early red. The purple BEAUTY, and the red NEW STONE, for bulk of crop. For very large ones of purple color, plant BUCKEYE STATE; and for late red, the PARAGON.

29. Kinds for Canners.—They should see to it that their growers plant PERFECTION and FAVORITE for early, the NEW STONE and BEAUTY for medium and bulk of crop, and PARAGON for late. If they wish to get very desirable kinds for canning the fruit whole in bottles, let me commend the red ARISTOCRAT, the purple POTATO-LEAF, and the yellow GOLD BALL. See Paragraph 61.

30. Kinds for Catsups and Preserves. — For catsups, ROYAL RED, and for preserves, GOLD BALL.

31. Kinds to Grow Under Glass.—I recommend for red color, THE PERFECTION and THE ARISTOCRAT; and for purple, THE ACME and THE BEAUTY.

Now, although we thus name these kinds for special purposes, yet the grower may profitably try other kinds if it suits his convenience better to do so. This list is largely intended for beginners, and is to have a general application.

32. Sowing Seed for Family Use.—Make a shallow tray or box two feet long, one foot wide, and six inches deep; or get a goods box from your grocer about the same size; or whatever will fit best into the sunniest window of the warmest room in your house. Take some rich black soil, with enough sand in it to keep it from baking after it is watered, and so it will make it warmer; put it first into the oven and heat it until all the weed seeds and insect life there may be in it will be destroyed, and then put into your box enough of it to fill the tray three-fourths full. Arrange to fix your box on such an incline at the window as to get the sun's rays perpendicularly, or square against the surface of the ground. Moisten this soil and stir in the sun from time to time, for a day or two, until it is in fine condition to make the seed germinate. All this is to be got ready from the middle of February to the middle of March in the latitude of Ohio; north or south of this, vary the time to suit. In this box plant the choicest seeds of the best kinds at your command. Lay it off in rows across the short way of the box, four inches apart, and if you wish to take the trouble, put the seeds about one-quarter inch apart in the row; otherwise sprinkle along, so as to be as near that thick in the row as you can hit it in that way; then cover with one-half or three-quarters of an inch of earth, and "*firm it down*" on the seed. Care must·be taken where two or more kinds are planted in the same box, to mark the rows carefully where they were planted, on the outside of the box, at the end of the rows; otherwise it will be forgotten which is which, by the time they are to be transplanted. Each kind should be set by themselves in the garden, and their names preserved throughout the season; then the grower will know which kinds suit him best, and so can tell what to send for next year. After the seed has been planted a day or two, dip a piece of brown paper or cloth in water, as warm as you would wish to put your hand in, and spread it over the whole surface of the ground. This covering should be remoistened in warm water every day or two, but especial care must be taken to remove it when the little tomato plants begin to "get their backs up" through the soil, which you may expect in a week or ten days after sowing. Stir the surface of the soil between the rows from time to time, and moisten just enough to keep the plants growing nicely, but not enough to force them along. They would better be too dry than too wet. The dryer the warmer, the less liable to rot, or to grow too fast, and be long, slim, weak plants. Keep them from getting stunted, but have them grow as short and stubby as you can get them. Transplanting will effect them less disastrously then when they go out into the world.

When they are two inches high prepare another

similar box to the one used at first, or boxes as may
be needed. Make the plants very wet, then raise
or pry them out so as to retain as much of the dirt upon
the roots as possible, and set them out again in rows
two inches apart and two inches from each other in the
row. Be sure to keep the different kinds separate, so
you will know which from which. When these plants
get to crowding each other, or about four or five
inches high, pass a sharp knife midway between
the plants on each side. This, if you have followed directions carefully, will give you a little plot two inches
square to each plant, and this plant will stand exactly
in the middle of it. Make them wet as before, and reset three or four inches apart, rowed both ways. If the
square plat of dirt is taken with the roots, they will
hardly know they were moved. As· they grow pass
the sharp knife midway between the rows at least
once in two weeks, to keep the roots from interlock-
ing, and to hold back the plants from growing too
tall. Some extra plants can be set in flower pots if need
be, scattered about the house wherever most convenient,
and best for them to grow. Aim to raise at least three
or four times as many as you need. If you do not need
them, your neighbors will want such plants at five or ten
cents apiece. But do you say, " This is a great deal of
bother?" Well, no; I do not think so. Suppose you
take fifty or seventy-five plants over the training I have
suggested, the sum total of your labor is not very great,
and when the fruits come on weeks before home grown
tomatoes are seen on the market, you will have your

rewards in the satisfaction of having what few others will have, and of eating refreshing fruit when you want it most.

As soon as the danger of frosts is past, transplant in the open garden. Let me suggest that, on all warm days before you set the plants in the garden, to open the window, or place them on the porch where the sun is warm; this gets them used to out-door life, but you must not forget for a single time to leave them out, and let the frosts nip them some cold night, or you will awaken in the morning to look upon the result with regrets for such careless loss of labor.

HARDENING TOMATO PLANTS.

"What is gained by starting plants early, and by frequent transplanting, can easily be lost again by neglecting to harden the plants off properly before their final transfer to the open ground. In fact, this is the most prolific source of disappointment and failure in getting the crop as early as the fine plants promised.

"The transfer from in-door protection to out-door exposure is always attended with risks, and generally results in a check to plant growth, from which the victims will not recover in weeks. Plants grown in hot beds or greenhouses should always be transferred to cold frames and left entirely without sash protection for a considerable time before they are set out in the open ground.

"The wise man always abides his time. Don't let your impatience hurry you and induce you to bed out plants before the ground has become thoroughly warmed through. The check is not owing to root mutilation or disturbance (as such would be beneficial rather than otherwise), but to change of atmospheric surroundings, soil, temperature, etc. The plant accustomed to hardships by previous exposure will suffer but little by the change."—*Farm and Fireside.*

For different methods of cultivation in the garden, see Paragraphs 45 to 49, inclusive. If you do not wish to grow the plants for yourself, reliable seedsmen will furnish them cheaply by express. This is a good way to get good plants, of good kinds, when you need them.

33. Common Hotbeds.—It will be necessary for all who wish to raise more tomatoes than they desire for their own use, to think of it in the fall of the year preceding that when they would raise the crop, in order to make the proper provisions for it. A warm, sunny spot should be chosen, on the south or southeast of buildings or other protection from north or northwest winds. Indeed, if these are not conveniently situated the grower should build a tight board fence eight or ten feet high, on the north and west sides of the place where he wishes to locate his hotbeds. These ought to be put as close to this fence as possible, and leave room to walk around between the fence and the beds. One thing must not be overlooked in the choice of a site for a hotbed, viz.: If the subsoil is porous it will not need drainage, but if it holds water the hotbed must be located so as to underdrain with ordinary three-inch tiles.

The best way to make these beds is to excavate the soil, with their length running east and west, for a depth of two feet, in the fall before frosts harden the ground. Drive a stout stake 2x2 or 2x3 inches carefully in each of the corners. Nail to these, on the outside, boards so the bed will be eighteen inches high on the north side and six inches high on the south side, and slope the ends to meet the sides so enclosing it. Bank up the north side and the ends with the dirt thrown out. If you buy

HOTBED.   HOTBED SASH.

sash expressly for the purpose (which you can of almost any first-class seedsman), it ought to be three feet by six feet in size, as this is probably the most convenient. Of course any kind of sash can be used, but in any case the size of the hotbed must be made to fit the sash used over it; and any size of hotbed can be made as desired, but almost the universal practice is to make them about six feet wide, and as long as will secure as many square feet of hotbed space as is needed.

Now we have the hole dug out, boarded around, and the earth banked up to it, and this done in the fall preceding; but you are not through with it yet. Put

into the bottom of it enough good black, or rich tan-
colored soil (having sand in it to loosen and make it
warm) to fill it seven inches deep.   On this throw in
and "firm down" enough fresh manure from the stable
to keep this good soil and the inside of the hotbed from
freezing until it is needed, about the middle of February
or first of March.   On some sunny day when this time
arrives, remove this manure, piling it out on all sides
except on the south side; also take out the good soil,
placing it on the south side of the bed, exercising care
to pulverize it as fine as possible in the handling of it.
Now put into this vacant bed eighteen inches of fresh
manure from the stable, that which will produce the
greatest heat, and tramp it down tightly, and make it
as level on the surface as you can.   If the manure is too
dry to heat, make it wet with hot water.   Spread on
top of this manure the rich soil six inches deep.   To get
it evenly spread, you must put on the whole six inches
as you go.   If you put two inches on, and then some
more, and then more, you will get it in uneven thick-
nesses and it will not work so well.   Now place the
glass over it, and, in a day or two, as soon as it gets warm
and dry, it is ready for the seed.

34. Sowing Seed in the Hotbed.—Make little
furrows on the surface of the bed, one inch deep and
three inches apart.   This will make the entire surface
into little ridges and hollows.   Sow your seed broadcast
upon the bed thus prepared, so it will contain about two
hundred and fifty seeds to the square foot.   Then take

your garden rake, turn it teeth upwards, and with the
back of it on the surface, lightly and diagonally draw it
over the ridges until it is all level again. Nearly all the
plants will then come up in rows. This plan saves
much time and many back aches. The soil should be
"*firmed down*" on the seed as soon as you have it in the
ground. This is done conveniently with a board of
suitable size, and your weight put on it; or with a small,
heavy hand roller. When small quantities of various
kinds are sown, the ordinary method of sowing a row
at a time should be observed. Be sure to mark carefully
where you have planted this kind or that, so that you can
know what you are planting out later in the season.
Do not depend on memory; mark it, so you will *know*.
Care must be taken now to keep the hotbed the right
temperature. It will be advisable for beginners to use
a thermometer, although persons of experience can tell
by merely putting their hand under the sash. If it gets
above 90° F. it is too hot, or below 50° F. it is too cold.
A range from sixty to eighty degrees will be right. If
the bed gets too hot, raise the sash, and equalize the
heat by letting in the outside air; but if this does not
cool the soil, and it is still too hot for the plants, then,
about each square yard, push down into the manure below, a stick like a broom-handle, remove carefully, and
pour in a bucketfull of cold water to each hole. And,
likewise, if the manure does not make it hot enough,
pour into such holes hot water instead of cold. The
heat may be increased, after the seed is planted, by removing the manure and some soil from about the out-

side of the beds, and packing them all around with fresh, hot manure from the stable.

You may expect the seed to come up in eight or ten days. Keep all weeds out; stir the soil with a weeder

WEEDERS.

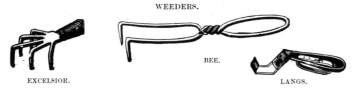

EXCELSIOR.   BEE.   LANGS.

once a week, and keep only wet enough to make plants grow well, but not so as to force them, or you will get long, slim plants where you need stalky, short, thick, stout ones. Keep the sash open as much as is prudent on warm days, whether the sun shines, or it is raining. It makes the plants healthier and accustoms them more certainly to the conditions of the out-door life they must lead a little later on.

35. More Extended Hotbeds.—These may also be necessary where it is desirable to go into the business of raising plants for market, or where the grower wishes more permanent arrangements than the common hotbeds ; or where he wishes to raise, as in the hothouse, other crops under glass before he needs to plant the seeds for tomatoes. These may be made more or less costly, as opportunity and means, or taste, may show to be wise. The site should be chosen in a place with good drainage, protected on the north and west, and having the sun shining upon it all day long. The length of the building should run, not east and west like the common

hotbed, but north and south like the hothouse. They
may be constructed of quarry stone, second-hand brick,
or of any lumber at hand and which may be suitable for
the purpose. Excavate to the depth of two or two and
a half feet, and seven feet wide, and to any length to
give the desired amount of surface. Wall up the sides
to four inches above the surface of the ground on
each side, and each end to a point, in the center, corres-
ponding to the comb of the house. For rafters use
strips of some good hard wood three inches wide and
one inch thick, and a little longer than the sash to be
used ; and it should be, say, three by four feet; then
each rafter would be four feet and three inches long.
These rafters should be cut in the ordinary way, only to
go up edgewise thus,

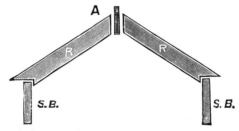

r. r.—Rafters, which are exactly equal in size.
s. b.—A section of the side-boards, an end view, on which the rafters rest for a plate.

Enough of the rafter should extend above the side-
boards to be a little above the sash, which is also to rest
on the side-board at the lower ends, and constitute a
main part of the roof. Between the rafters at the top
is to be nailed in a strip one inch square (see cut as at

a), and long enough to reach two inches above the tip-top point of the comb. This two inches is to be whittled to a three-quarters inch round. Upon them is to be dropped a strip three inches wide and one thick, having holes bored to suit, to act as a ridgepole. A set of these rafters is to go at each end, and a pair between each pair of sash, which comb upon each other at the top, just under the ridgeboard, while the lower ends lie on the upper edge of the side-boards. To adjust the sash, drive a stiff wire nail with a flat, thin head, through the rafter into the side of the sash, about eighteen inches from the top, on each side of it. This makes a perfect hinge. Then the next pair are fastened in, say, nineteen inches from the top, in the same way; and your building is complete. There ought to be a little slide door, or ventilator, in each end. When the grower wishes to work in this hotbed, by having a stick about a yard long, and loosely hinged with a staple at the bottom end of sash, he can quickly adjust it at any angle desired. If he bores holes in it, and in the rafters to correspond, he can, with a pin, set the sash perpendicularly, or at any angle, in order to let in a warm spring shower so as to save much labor in watering his plants. He can thus regulate the temperature of this house also. One advantage over the common hotbed is that you can work it from each side, and never have to handle the sash except to raise and lower them.

Prepare for these hotbeds and plant in them the same as already described in Paragraphs 32 and 33. In these houses crops of lettuce, radishes, cucumbers, or other things could be grown before needed for tomatoes. If desired for winter crops, especially of tomatoes, by lengthening the sash, excavating in the earth deeper, and introducing artificial heat, a profitable hothouse can be very cheaply constructed in this way.

36. A Circular Hothouse.—I have never tried it, but I have often thought about a Circular Hothouse, which seemed to me might be very profitable, where a man had the material at hand and could do most of the work himself in building it. Locate the house on a warm southern slope, with an incline of thirty degrees to the east. Excavate on the upper side, throwing the earth down hill, sufficient to secure a circular level place thirty feet in diameter. Excavate still deeper for a furnace below the level, in the center of this plat, and wall up to the surface; also wall up a way out to the south on a level with the furnace room floor. Directly over the furnace construct a hothouse bed in a circle with a diameter of eight feet. Around this conduct a walk of two feet in width, and around this again, construct plant beds seven feet in width; and then another walk of two feet all around this. Cover the whole with glass and sash; and also near the sides with glazed sash three feet by three feet. The entrance to it must be from the entry to furnace room, by a stair leading up under the seven-foot bed, in opposite directions, to the walks. If it can be located below a spring of water, the water needed can be conducted through the building by pipes, and be most convenient. This house will, no

doubt, cost more to construct than one in the form of a
rectangle with square corners; and yet the advantages
of heating, watering, and working this one would pay
well for it.

37. Cold Frames.—These are made like common
hotbeds (see Paragraph 33), only not so deep nor having so much manure—ten inches is enough—in them
under the soil, so it is not necessary to dig out so deep
for them; these are covered with glass, or what is much
cheaper and more easily handled, they may be covered
with hotbed oiled cloth, or "Plant Bed Cloth," as seeds-

PLANT BED CLOTH.

men call it. By tacking it to light frames, three feet
wide by six feet long, they can be used most handily.
These cold frames are for receiving the plants when the
grower first transplants them from the hotbeds, or resets
them again to keep them "stalky." It also gives them
more room to grow, and as it is not so warm, the plants
are got a little hardier for out-door life when the frosts
come on no more.

The plants should be lifted out with a garden
trowel, put into a shallow tray, and "*pricked out*" with a
dibble, or angle transplanting trowel, into the cold frame
as described in Paragraph 32. They should be set three
or four inches apart, and rowed straight both ways. They

grow well, and work easily this way with the hand weeder (see cut). This makes it possible, also, to prune the roots by passing a knife midway between the plants, each way of the rows, about once a week, with the re-

CLEVES ANGLE TRANSPLANTING TROWEL.   DIBBLE.

sult of keeping the plants short and stout. It is an advantage, too, when the final transplanting comes, as you can take this earthen cube of three or four inches dimensions along with the plant, and it will hardly recognize that it has gone "out into the world," and can now make the most of itself without any great hindrance in " getting started in life."

GARDEN TROWEL.

I wish to remark here, that whoever labors at this kind of work should constantly study what conditions are best for his plants throughout all the changes they must make: and also, how he can most cheaply and conveniently afford them these good conditions. In one

sentence, study to do the best things easiest; for labor,
time, or expense, saved habitually, is almost equivalent
to cash in hand.

For Southern growers, I want to make a suggestion
in regard to Cold Frames: only for them they should be
called Heat Frames; for as the former is against cold in
the North, so in the South could they be used against
heat. Especially would this advantage appear in raising
an early crop in winter. Locate this Frame in a somewhat shaded, cool place. If the natural shade cannot
be found, then make it artificially of lumber, brush,
cloth, or anything at hand. No manure is needed; just
level off the place, drive the stakes, nail up the boards,
bank up the dirt to the boards, and cover with "Plant-
bed Cloth." Put in good soil in which to sow the seed,
and plant it in July or August. Open at night, but
cover in the day-time. If it is very hot weather, and
liable to burn them, saturate the soil all around the bed
with cold water. In this way an earlier winter crop can
be grown; for now Southern growers must wait till the
weather is cool enough "out o' doors" to grow their
plants, and so lose much good trade they could by these
means otherwise attain.

For Canners, or those who grow for them, no hot
bed is needed, only these Cold Frames for earliest, as one
transplanting will answer. Large growers find time
only for this or resetting. They plant enough later so
that the weather is not cold enough to demand more
heat than these afford. Indeed, many of these growers
sow the seed in drills in the open field, in rich soil, about

the middle of April, and reset from these rows in the field. The risk is too great. It would pay better to build and use the Cold Frames. The latest crop might be risked this way, by planting the first of May. The Cold-Frames are an advantage because they are the means by which plants acquire age without growing tall and spindling, and so bear earlier after they are set out in the field, and are less stunted by the transfer. The importance of "stalky" plants cannot be over-estimated. However, if your plants do get too tall and slender by the time you dare risk them "out o' doors," do not throw them away, but do one of two things: either pull them and "*heel them in*," as fruit men say of trees—that is, put them in bunches of twenty-five or fifty, and cover the roots in the ground; water well, and when it is well soaked away cover plants with dry earth pretty well up on the stalks. Or you can let them grow and then transplant, by letting the stalk lie along in the furrow, covering it with about the same depth of earth as commonly sets a plant, and leaving only so much of the top above ground as can "hold up its head." It will not do to set them deep in the ground, as they will rot off; but as above, it is an advantage, because at the joints roots will grow out and feed the plant more than common, and force it faster than otherwise. Indeed, some growers urge this as the best way to get an early and productive crop.

Cold Frames for an acre, with plants set as directed above, viz.: three inches each way from each other, would require to be thirty feet long by six feet wide, or its equivalent in shorter beds. To put it in round numbers, an ounce of tomato seed has twenty-five hundred seeds; by this you can calculate how much seed you will want, and how much hotbed space it will take to grow your plants. Never depend on just barely enough to go around. No telling what may happen. Calculate for abundance of plants.

38. Preparation of Soil in the Field for the Plants.—Tomatoes can be grown wherever corn could be planted. Crops will vary also in proportion to the productiveness of the soil. Select a field of sandy black loam or rich tan-colored clayey soil. To get the best fruits, land that is rich enough to fetch fifty to seventy-five bushels of corn to the acre should be chosen. Plow under a clover sod in the fall, or if possible in February, so it will get a good freeze or two. If the clover sod cannot be had, then take the next best field, viz.: the second crop after clover. I prefer for tomatoes to improve the land by "clovering" above all other kinds of fertilizers. Next to clover I use *well-rotted* stable manure. In order to get it well rotted I pitch it over in the early spring, at least once a month. By piling it over itself two or three times it will not burn itself out by its own heat and be almost useless, nor yet will it leach out with rains falling on it. For any crop where stable manure is used, this is a most important point. It can not be out of place here to say, no man can afford to go from year to year without a large saucer-shaped space, with one side of it near his barn, where he throws out his manures, so that as it heaps up he can pile it over,

and so on, to the other side, when he will have a heap of compost which would delight the eye of any man intelligent enough to know its commercial value. This shallow basin ought to be three times as large as necessary to hold the manure, and cemented, or have clay that will hold water well pounded in all over the bottom of it.

If the grower fertilizes with this for a tomato crop, let him spread on broadcast over his land a heavy coat— from one to four inches—and plow it under in the spring. If the land was plowed in the fall, no matter, plow again. No crop is hurt by thorough plowing and plenty of pulverizing before the plants are set in the ground. Of course commercial fertilizers can be used to advantage, but it can be applied best when transplanting or growing, and they will be described in place. In a word, whatever will thoroughly prepare a rich field in good shape for any common crop, will be all right for tomatoes.

39. The Marker.—When it comes time to put the plants into the open field you will be in a hurry, and you will find it very advisable to prepare for it previously, during any leisure time you may have in the winter. A Marker will be needed, and I here submit a plan for one, which I used for a good many years. It is made like a sled with plank runners, only it has four runners instead of two, and they are thicker and shorter than usual for sleds, and set four feet apart—"r" is the runner, made of pine or other lumber. They should be three feet long, six inches wide, and three inches thick. "Sc" is a scantling, two by four inches, and a little over

twelve feet long. It should set into the upper edge of
the runners, about three inches back from the front end,
to the depth of one or one and a half inches, and be
spiked down firmly. On the rear ends nail a strong
board, one inch thick and fourteen wide, having same
length as scantling (see "B" in cut). Any blacksmith
can make hinges or clips, as at "c" "c" in cut, to receive
a tongue for hitching a team to it. A good way to do
is to find some tongue or "pole" belonging to an old
spring wagon no longer used, then it can be left in all

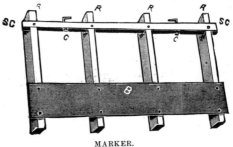

MARKER.

the time, and the marker is always ready the year around.
It is not an unhandy conveyance to have around anyhow,
as it can be used for many things, such as moving plows,
harrows, and even stones or other rubbish, wherever
desired. The driver, when using it for a marker, usually
stands on the broad board, and drives across the field,
and by using stakes secures straight rows.

Now, from the tenth to the twentieth of May, or
after you are satisfied that danger from frosts and real
cold nights are past, and having your ground well plowed
and harrowed, take the marker, and driving to stakes

set in the ordinary way, make rows as straight as possible across the field. This will give four rows "*at a through,*" and so mark out your ground pretty rapidly. By using a shovel plow, or similar implement, draw furrows across these markings from two feet to seven, as may be needed. For Dwarf Champion, Aristocrat, any tree-like kinds, or any variety for training or stalking up, from two to three feet will be wide enough to furrow out the ground. Acme and Potato Leaf may be furrowed from three to four feet apart, while all other varieties for "down-culture" will need to be placed from four to seven feet apart. The kind, the tendency to vine, and the strength of the soil, must decide how far plants should be set apart. One thing is certain, there is far more danger of getting them too close than too far from each other in the field. It looks like a great waste of land to set plants seven feet apart, but it will pay to do it on rich soil, and for the best kinds. If the tops interlap or overlap each other, much injury is done the crop. When in New Jersey and Delaware among the canners this last fall, 1892, I found that their Paragon Tomatoes (noted everywhere for its adaptability for a late crop) were all intertwined and overlapped, and I feel sure it was the cause of a complaint that the tomatoes were small on the "last pickings." No one expects to get six stalks of good corn in each hill; neither should he if he plants two stalks of tomatoes where only one should be. Some growers plant "First in Market Peas," or other quickly maturing crop, between the rows, and so save something of this apparent waste of land. Let me suggest, also, that the grower do not mark off more ground than he can set out while it is still fresh and moist in the furrows. If they get rained on and dried hard in the sun, run the shovel plow through again in the furrow. It will do no harm, if your ground is a little hard or cloddy, to run a second time in each furrow anyhow. It affords more fine dirt for transplanting. If you wish to use commercial fertilizers, secure and have ready in the field at this juncture, put into the crossing of your marking out about a gill, and hoe it in a little with a common hoe. A complete fertilizer for a tomato crop, to be sowed broadcast and harrowed in, is as follows: Dried ground fish, 833 lbs.; dissolved bone black, 210 lbs.; muriate of potash, 150 lbs. Stated in per cents, it would be: Nitrogen 5, phosphoric acid 10, potash 8. A 1,000 lbs. per acre will be needed. It should be put on the day before the plants are set in the ground. In general, fertilizers mostly nitrogen and potash seem best suited for the tomato. On rich soils, use less nitrogen and more potash, as a rule. From Semper's "Manures," on pages 149 and 150, I quote the following fertilizers for tomatoes per acre:

No. 1. Nitrate of soda, ... 200 lbs.
        Dried blood, ... 100 "
        Cotton seed meal, . . . 300 ·"
        Dissolved bone-black, . . . 400 "
        Dissolved South Carolina rock, . . 400 "
        Muriate of Potash, ... 100 "

            GEORGIA EXPERIMENTAL STATION.

No. 2. Nitrate of soda, ... 400 lbs.
        Superphosphate, ... 800 "
        Muriate of potash, ... 200 "

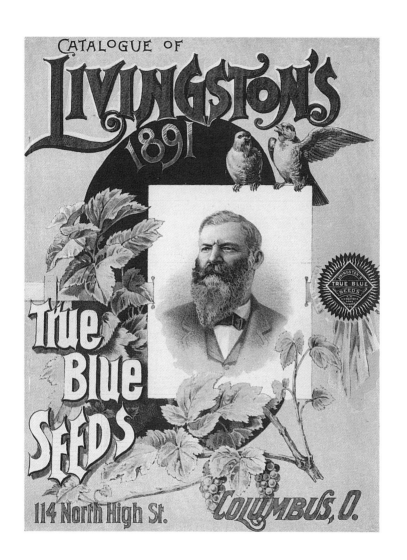

CATALOGUE OF

LIVINGSTON'S
1891

True Blue SEEDS

114 North High St.

COLUMBUS, O.

LIVINGSTON'S

OHIO'S
1888
CENTENNIAL

BUCKEYE GARDEN

SEEDS

ORIGINATORS OF

LIVINGSTON'S
BEAUTY,
ACME
PARAGON,
PERFECTION
FAVORITE,
GOLDEN QUEEN
&
POTATO LEAF
TOMATOES,
&c. &c.

LIVINGSTON'S NEW BEAUTY.

A. W. LIVINGSTON'S SONS,
111 N. High Street, Columbus, Ohio.

Livingston's 1889

ORIGINATORS
OF
LIVINGSTON'S
BEAUTY,
ACME,
PARAGON,
PERFECTION
FAVORITE,
GOLDEN QUEEN,
POTATO LEAF,
TOMATOES
&c. &c.

LIVINGSTON'S
New Beauty.

BUCKEYE GARDEN SEEDS

A.W. LIVINGSTON'S SONS.
143 NORTH HIGH STREET.
COLUMBUS, OHIO.

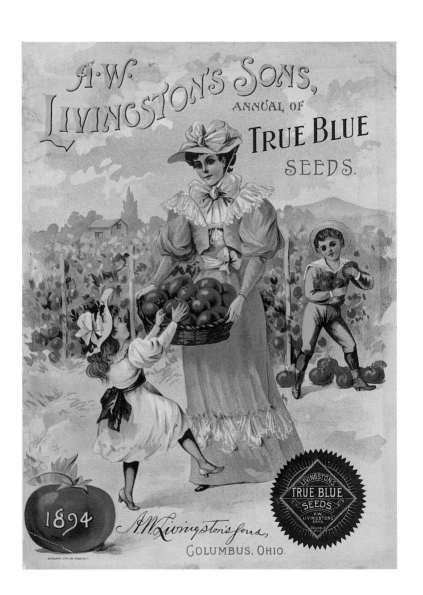

A·W· LIVINGSTON'S SONS, ANNUAL OF TRUE BLUE SEEDS.

1894

A. W. Livingston's Sons,
COLUMBUS, OHIO.

LIVINGSTON'S TRUE BLUE SEEDS. A. W. LIVINGSTON'S SONS. COLUMBUS, OHIO.

TRUE 1907 BLUE

The
LIVINGSTON
SEED CO.

ANNVAL BOOK of
SEEDS PLANTS
& BVLBS

COLVMBVS, O.
V.S.A.

LIVINGSTON'S
HVMMER
TOMATO
ROUND AS A BALL—
BRIGHT SCARLET, GOOD FORCER
VERY PROLIFIC

Packet 20¢   3 Packets 50¢   7 Packets $1.00

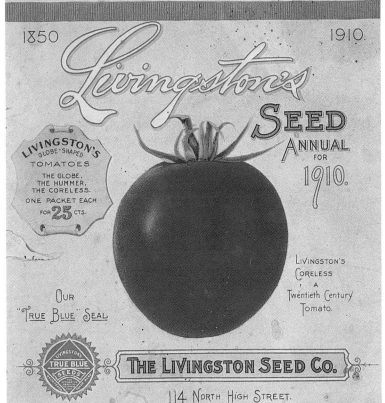

Sixtieth Anniversary Edition

1850   1910.

Livingston's

SEED
ANNUAL
FOR
1910.

LIVINGSTON'S
GLOBE-SHAPED
TOMATOES
THE GLOBE,
THE HUMMER,
THE CORELESS.
ONE PACKET EACH
FOR 25 CTS.

LIVINGSTON'S
CORELESS
A
Twentieth Century
Tomato.

OUR
"TRUE BLUE" SEAL

LIVINGSTON'S
TRUE BLUE
SEEDS

THE LIVINGSTON SEED CO.

114 NORTH HIGH STREET.
COLUMBUS, OHIO.

Stands for Highest Quality.

Livingston's Seed Annual
FOR
1920

ESTABLISHED
1850

LIVINGSTON'S
TRUE BLUE
SEEDS

LIVINGSTON'S
MANYFOLD
TOMATO
PACKET........15¢

THE LIVINGSTON SEED Co.
"FAMOUS FOR TOMATOES"
114 NORTH HIGH ST., COLUMBUS. OHIO

Every grower ought to try different plant-foods for his crops till he learns what is best for his fields; but almost anywhere he may well try a gill of hard wood ashes to each plant, with good hope of increased harvests. Let me urge the grower to be thorough in all that he does. Do not be afraid of work. A little boy once said to his father:

"I know what makes these onions grow so well."

"Why, my son?"

"Because you have to get down on your knees so much to them."

The secret of successful gardening consists in attending diligently to your crop WHEN IT NEEDS IT.

40. Transplanting Into the Open Field.—Turn back to Paragraph 32 and read it over. During the winter previous make a "Handy Tray" for carrying plants. It is made of one-half inch lumber. It should be two

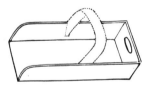

HANDY TRAY.

feet long, sixteen inches wide, and four deep. One end should be left out. In the other end a suitable hole is cut, so the hand can slip into it, for a handle, while the open end is caught by the bottom, and so is easily carried. Sometimes a strong wooden hoop is bended over in the middle from side to side, and makes a basket-like handle. A shallow goods box (made over a little) will answer very well. If each hand setting out plants carries a tray with him, then the handle is a disadvantage, for he drags his tray full of plants along the ground, and sets as he goes. If one drops plants and another sets them out, then the handle is an advantage, for he can carry it with one hand and drop with the other.

An hour or two before beginning the work of transplanting, or about one or two o'clock P. M., pass the knife between the plants midway between the rows each way, at least four inches deep; then wet the plants thoroughly and let the water soak into the ground for one or two hours. During this time enough furrowing out for that evening can be done. Then take trays enough to hold all the plants to be wet that evening. You will need a small mason's trowel, or better, "Cleaves' Steel Dibber," flat blade, two and a half inches by nine, having a spade-like handle.

FLAT BLADE DIBBER.   CLEVES ROUND DIBBER.

By using this in the cold frame, the three or four inch cubes of soil with a plant in its center can be taken out, one by one, and slipped off into the tray. Elevate the open end of the tray a little, and commencing at the closed end of it, pack in the plants till it is full. Care should be taken not to crush the soil from the roots in handling them.   As each tray is filled place in the wagon, and when sufficient number is obtained all hands are away to the field.

A careful way here is for each hand to take a tray, and following a row, slip the plants out into the furrow at the crossings, keeping them upright and as much soil about the rootlets as possible.   When in place, press some fine soil around the plant with the hand, so it will stand firmly.   It will not come amiss then to water each plant (about a pint to the plant), and the next morning go along with the hoe and hill up the dirt to it.   It will hardly know it is moved in this way, if they have been "hardened off" well (see Paragraph 32), and this will add to the earliness of your "earliest of all" at least a week.   Have a care, also, if you take different kinds in your trays, or in the same wagon-load, not to get them mixed up in setting them out.

Let me put in a warning against the use of "volunteer plants," or such as come up of their own accord in the spring on soil planted to tomatoes the year before. They cannot be depended on as true to kind, not even if the best of selected stock seed was used the year previous.   My crop was once destroyed by cut-worms, and I used some volunteer plants and had seed that produced all sorts.   I am often asked: "Why will not 'volunteers' come true to kind?"   I am not able fully to answer this question, but I have a theory which may help some one else to study it out.   It seems strange that it is so; indeed, it appears impossible, yet I know it is true.   It is worst in the South—in Florida, Mississippi, and else-

where—where frosts do not kill them out during the
winter. Things left to themselves get wild, degenerate,
"run out." Without coddling or nursing under the
most favorable circumstances for their growth, they keep
only the most hardy qualities, while the best and tender-
est parts retain only enough of themselves to sustain
life—that is, these parts run down to the lowest range
of limit and live. Hence the difference between a wild
native tomato and one of my improved smooth varieties.
I have no question but the best tomato on the markets
to-day, if left to itself for eight or ten years, would
"run out" or degenerate to the lowest point of its limitations; but that same tomato, if not crossed with other
kinds, could be brought up again (by observing to put
it under right conditions) to the highest point of exeel-
lence within its limitations. Hence it will be seen that
the stock-seed grower must be one who understands how
to "*keep up*" their excellencies, if the fruit-growers get
what they desire, and ought to have, from year to year.
Another reason lies in the fact, that if this is any kind
of tomato which has any original wild mixed blood in
it, lying out all winter is calculated to furnish the conditions for its development; and hence it appears, while
under the better or higher cultivation, such things would
continue latent, and might not be seen for years.

Coming back from this digression about "volunteers" to the matter of Transplanting again, another
way of handling the plants for field culture, especially
for large acreages, when so great care cannot be taken
for want of time, and because of expense of extra help,

is to let one hand take the tray on his arm and drop one
plant in each hill, with the tops all one way; then another can follow up, coming to the plant against its top
instead of its roots, and with his "Cleaves' Dibber" (or
similar implement) make a slanting hole in the soil in
the Rill, and lifting it, slip the tomato root in and let
the dirt fall back on the plant, giving it a little firming
down with his foot as he passes on.   With practice, boys
sixteen to twenty years old get to be experts in the use
of the dibber.   Afterwards apply the water, and hoe up
the next morning, as before described.   In this way
plants can be set out until the first of July for a general
crop.   Sometimes, if desirable, the seed can be planted

SOWING SEED.

in rows in some rich, waste soil in the open field, from
1st of May to the 15th of same month.   To transplant
these, wet the rows thoroughly two hours before pulling
them; pull, and set as described before in this paragraph,
but *always* put the water to them and hoe in the dry soil

after the water soaks away. Not many plants will be lost this way, but they will be stunted a little, and so will not bear fruit so early after transplanting as plants raised in hotbeds and brought up in the cold-frames. It is never necessary to wait for wet weather in order to transplant successfully. Plenty of water used in taking the plants up, and also in setting out again, insures a good supply of rootlets and good mingling of them in the ground again. If this is followed with the hoe or suitable cultivation almost at once, the results are more satisfactory than when one works in soil that is too wet, for then the soil is apt to bake, and sometimes hardens around a stalk and fairly girdles it.

Do not get nervous, and put your plants out too early. Nothing is gained by it. Cold rains, cold nights, danger of frosts, and shady days, injure them and destroy many plants. Wait till you feel you will have warm, growing weather, then stick them in. I have waited till the first of June for early here, and then came into market before others who had set out two or three weeks ahead of me. A good way to tell when it is safe to risk transplanting in the field, is to watch the buds on the oak trees, and when the leaves are like a squirrel's foot the time has come for first early to be set out in the field.

41. **Implements for Cultivation.**—These may be any ordinary implements for cultivating the soil, such as one has at hand and employs in other crops; but whatever is to be used should be on the ground, for cultiva-

tion must begin at once after the transplanting is finished
in the field. The Planet, Jr., implements are, all in all,
the best in the market, and can be bought of seedsmen
everywhere. The Planet, Jr., Horse Hoe and the Planet,
Jr., One-Horse Harrow, for surface and level cultivation,
are A No. 1.

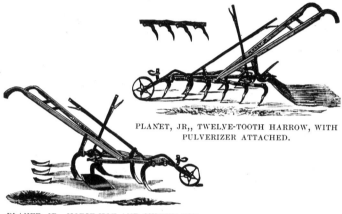

PLANET, JR,, TWELVE-TOOTH HARROW, WITH
PULVERIZER ATTACHED.

PLANET, JR., HORSE HOE AND CULTIVATOR
COMBINED.

42. Cultivation of Field Crop.—Tomatoes need
culture as soon after transplanting as possible, and after
that about once a week till the vines fall down and make
further cultivation impracticable. But even then, if the
season has been such as to allow big weeds to show
themselves above the plants, go through after a heavy
shower and pull them out by hand. The fine steel-
toothed one-horse harrow is best for level and first cultivation. The Planet, Jr., Cultivator will answer for
second and third cultivation. If marked out to sow

both ways of the field, and if at all convenient, work
the crop both ways alternately. Great care must be
taken not to disturb the roots after the plants fall down
or are in bloom. Very shallow culture is best after the
plants begin to spread out over the field. The same
general matters of importance in the culture of any
crop apply to raising tomatoes in their "down-cultiva-
tion" in the open field.

Work them well, keep the ground clear of weeds,
give them room to "*spread themselves*," and the grower
will not need to complain of results.

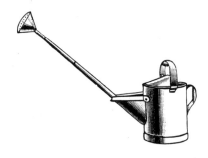

Other methods, more or less practical to some of my readers, deserve mention and description here. According to circumstances or desires of the growers, they have been employed to greater or less advantage. These are Staking up and Trellising in various ways, which are increasingly popular from season to season.

43. Mulching Tomatoes. — For down-culture, there may be added to the above methods of ordinary cultivation that of mulching the ground quite heavily under the vines with straw. This is especially desirable for a dry, sunny hillside location or for dry seasons, or in any kind of light soil that spatters up badly on the fruit, or in very weedy, foul ground. This is only practicable when one has the straw and not too large an acreage to cover. It is especially desirable to turn the vines a little along the rows, and, it may be, to trim the tops that seek to drop over to their neighbor's rows, so as to leave a comfortable and convenient walk between them to gather the fruit. Land is not generally so scarce as yet in America that we cannot afford to give our tomatoes plenty of room to grow all they want to, and so do us better service all around. Try some tomatoes with this straw mulch, and see how it works for you. 'If the season turns out wet, then draw the straw away from the roots and leave between the rows.

44. Pruning on Down-Culture. — If a grower has the time and working force to do it, there is real, substantial gain to pass along the rows, and when the side-shoots begin to appear select, say four, of the most vigorous and let these only grow—cut off all the rest. If you cut them off as fast as they get to be an inch or two long, you will get the best results out of the trimming. You will need to pass over them several times to get it best done, but you will like it in improved quality of fruits gained. Some also advocate cutting the ends of vines off after the tenth of September. This can be done as conveniently with a common hand cornknife as anything else, and may be worth a trial, although I cannot speak from any definite experiences of my own.

45. Staking up Tomatoes.—For a considerable crop, this method is being tried more and more, and the evidence of experience is in favor of it, where it can be done at all. In some of the Southern States their field crop is raised in this way. It is a most advantageous method for farmers, village, or city gardeners. The stakes may be poles of two or three inches growth and six to eight feet long, or sawed lumber of one inch thick by two or three wide, and the same length as above. These should be got ready during leisure time, the winter previous. After the second cultivation in the open field, or when the plants are twelve or fifteen inches high, just before they fall down and begin to spread out, put the stakes in the front end of a wagon or sled—not more than one-half a load. A wide-awake boy can drive the team straddle of the second row in the field. Two men, with an ax apiece, can set and drive them, one in the first and the other in the third row on each side of the conveyance, and by taking every other one they can also place a stake in the row at the rear of the vehicle. They can do this without getting out, and so set three rows "at a through," and with good speed. These stakes should, of course, be sharpened beforehand, and when left should stand quite firmly in the ground.

Another method of fixing these stakes in place, is to take a reasonably heavy crowbar of iron, having a sharp point and a swell above it to make a hole about same size as the stake to be set. By raising it up and forcing it into the ground a few times in the same place, a hole of sufficient size and depth will be made, so that when the stake is thrust into it solidly, and the earth tramped firmly about the surface with the feet, it will stand ready for service. An ax or sledge can also be used to drive a short stake with a ring of iron around the top to keep it from splitting, and when removed carefully the tall stake can be set in the hole, as described above. If any one has other methods which are handier for them, they will answer. The point to be attained is to get a stake from four to six feet above ground, which is strong enough, and set firm enough, to hold up a tomato vine in full bearing, and to get this ready and in the hill by the time the plant is ready to topple over on the ground.

46. Tying up to the stake is done by using some soft twine, jute, or raffia, which can be bought of seedsmen at a few cents a pound, although any kind of string will answer if not so fine and hard as to cut the plant.

With this tie *loosely* around the plant and *tightly* around the stake one foot from the ground; again tie at two feet high, and another at three feet, and another at four, and, if necessary, another at five; but the last tying should be made firm to the plant, because the heavy fruit must be sustained; yet this last tying should also be above where the fruit "*sets*" on the vines. Here let me say, that some of the objects of "staking up" are to get larger, cleaner, smoother, better flavored fruits, and especially an earlier, and a larger number of choice, marketable fruits to the vine. Many, therefore, when about five to eight clusters have set on each stalk, do not let more grow on it, but while pruning trim them off, and throw the strength of the vine into these clusters. They claim that this brings quicker and more "earliest of all" than ordinary culture. This necessitates "Pruning," which we will describe in the next paragraph.

Another method of "tying up," especially if you have flat stakes, is to take a piece of braid, or a strip of cloth or leather, three-quarters inch wide and four to six inches long. Give it one turn around the plant, and drive a tack through the two ends lapped over each other and into the stake, at each foot of its growth. If two shoots are allowed to grow, tack on opposite sides of the stake, so as to fasten a shoot on each side. Here again anything will answer that holds the plant up to the stake and does not injure the growth of the vine. I might say, for Western men who will likely want to use pine board stakes, dip the part of the stake that goes into the ground, and a foot more of it, into hot, strong brine, having a pint of tar to every two gallons of brine, put into it when hot. It will help, too, to put into it a little crude carbolic acid, also a little cheap oily matter, like crude petroleum. This is a cheap decoction which will go a long way, and pay well in preserving your stakes. Stakes should be piled up in a dry shed when not in use.

Another thing, if only a few clusters are allowed to grow on a vine, then a succession of plants should be set every two weeks until the fourth of July, so as to have others coming on after these all ripen. The last set out will be in the first flush for ripening about the time frosts come, so that quite a goodly lot can be held to ripen in a dry, sunny cellar, or shed which is frost-proof, and will sell to advantage.

All kinds of fancy "*staking up*" for beauty or profit will afford pleasure for those who have a taste for such crops, and pay well. If one wishes to see how much fruit he can make a single stalk bear, and have for his labor something that will attract his neighbor's attention as he passes by, let him, for each plant, dig a hole not less than two and a half feet square and two deep. Fill it with rich soil mixed in equal parts with thoroughly well-rotted manure. As this compost is put in, "*firm* it" around a strong post to stand six or eight feet out of the ground, and nail to it any arrangements of bars, straight or curved, or hoops in any shape or form to suit the grower's fancy, and then train by tying up a good supply of the strongest branches, as before described. By nailing strong wooden hoops, such as are found on

sugar barrels, about two feet in diameter, to the two
opposite sides of the post, as shown in the illustration,
a "tree-tomato" can be made which will delight the eyes
of all who see it. For the top and bottom hoops, cut
into the side of post about one-quarter of an inch, then

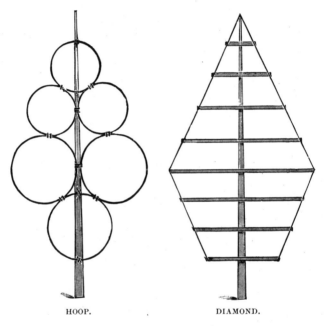

HOOP.   DIAMOND.

by cutting them in two they can be toe-nailed into the
post and so fastened firmly, and also match the others.
The vines should follow the hoops and leave the clusters
open, also let them cross where the hoops touch. The
smaller hoops are made by cutting apart and overlapping.
The fancy grower may, if he prefers, have something

very pretty by nailing hard-wood plastering lath, or similar strips of any kind of wood, in such lengths as to
make a diamond form. Two strong fence wires should
pass and be stapled around the outer ends of the cleats,
as near an inch apart as may be. Train the shoots out
on these like a grape-vine, and keep well trimmed.
Many other forms might be given and used—in fact,
anything desired.

47. Training or Pruning Tomatoes.—Within a
few days after, or at the time of first tying up to the
stakes or trellis, pass along the rows, select one, or two
at most, of the thriftiest and most promising shoots on
the vine and let these grow. Pinch or cut all the other
sprouts off, and do this as often as is necessary, to keep
the whole strength of the plant growing into these
shoots. It will be needed about once a week. Some
growing on rich ground trim off a portion of the leaves,
keeping only enough to shade duly the fruits from the
hot, scorching suns which occur after summer showers.

A successful grower, of twenty-three years experience, gives his methods as follows: "I have a garden spot
fifty by sixty-four feet in size; but from it I furnish my
family of ten, with all the vegetables they need; and sell
from $25 to $30 worth off surplus. Tomatoes are my
hobby, and I have the reputation of raising the finest in
the market. I gained this by using your kinds, and the
methods I here describe of cultivating them : I first
prepare my ground by removing the soil for several
feet, put into the trench two feet of manure well tramped

down, then six inches of soil, and then eight inches of well-rotted manure, and soil again till I reach the surface. In such a soil, cut-worms and grubs bred, and cut off a great deal I planted. Angle worms honey-combed this soil so that it dried out like an ash heap, as the dry weather came on; and tomato worms added their work of destruction on the tender growths I thus secured. Experience had taught me however, that tomatoes love a rich soil; so I worked to keep this, and still get rid of the pests, and I have succeeded.. For two years I have not lost a plant by the worms, and my neighbors not using my methods have lost heavily by the ravages of these vermin. My remedy is, ' To one bushel of air-slaked lime and one bushel un-leached ashes, add ten pounds of salt; mix well and cover over the ground an inch deep, then dig deep with a spading fork and work into the soil at the same time more well-rotted manure. Then cover the surface again with one-half inch of the lime, ash and salt mixture and rake it in thoroughly with the garden rake.' This mixture is a good fertilizer, thus used with the manure, and is at the same time obnoxious to the pests that work in the soil. I sow my seed in hot-beds about the middle of March, and carefully harden my plants by keeping the sash off whenever possible, and set out my plants as early in May as is safe—two and one-half feet apart each way. Into each hill I stick a pole or board one by two inches and eight feet long. When plants are eight or ten inches high, tie up to the pole. When they throw out branches I select three or four of the

TRAINING OR PRUNING TOMATOES.

strongest shoots and pinch off all the rest; and continue
to pinch them off, but tie the others up as they grow.
I trim out enough leaf-limbs so that the fruit is not
crowded and to get air and sun enough for it. About
the tenth of September, I cut off the top. By this severe
trimming, the sap is thrown into the fruit, and the sun
and the air will ripen it in almost any weather. I mulch
the ground well with saw dust around the vines. While
in number I may not get as many tomatoes, as if left to
run at will, but I get far more weight and the quality is
far superior. On his own offer, a grocer paid me in
cash, double the price he could get them for from market
gardeners, and told me he made more out of them,
as he could sell all I could let him have at his own
price and sell easier than others, though he did not
charge so much for them."

I give the above in full from an Illinois grower, to
show how it confirms the positions we have taken, and
also how well it will pay to do the careful work necessary to secure these results. It is likely this grower
would have succeeded quite as well, and, I think better,
to have trained two stalks up the stake and let two run
over the ground at will. Although by tying loosely for
all the tyings, but the last one, and letting the stalks
swing out, a little apart in different directions from the
stake, it is not astonishing that he got such fine crops
of tomatoes and call it a decided success. Some also
add to the above, bagging (as grapes are.)

There is no reason why those who live in cities or
towns, as well as farmers, might just as well as not have

all the nice tomatoes they can eat. A half dozen stalks fixed and worked as described above, will produce all any family can eat.

48. Growing Tomatoes in Barrels.—This is a method strongly recommended in the *American Agriculturist* a few years ago. For early fruit, place a barrel as large as a coal-oil barrel, in a warm corner about the buildings. Let it down in the ground about one-third its height. Do not forget to bore three or four inch auger holes in the bottom to let the water out. When the barrel is well packed in, fill it half full of fresh, hot stable manure and tramp it down tightly. Pour a bucket full—two gallons—of hot water upon this manure, then put on good soil eight inches, then a mixture of well-rotted manure and rich, black loam in about equal quantities, until you reach about eight to twelve inches of the top of the barrel, then heap manure around outside. Set three plants in this and trim to two shoots each. Train one of these each up on stakes or on buildings near by. For the other three I advise to take a strip of cloth about six inches wide, spread it over straw wadded around the barrel's chime and tack it fast, then let the latter shoots grow out over this cushion and run at will. Be careful to give these plenty of water. A gallon each day will not be too much. Three or four old barrels set around in odd corners which are likely to be otherwise unimportant will furnish enough tomatoes, and a variety at that, to supply a family of five for a whole year.

49. Trellising Tomatoes.—During the winter, prepare stakes—preferably board one or one and a quarter inches thick, three wide and four to seven feet long— as tall kinds or fruitfulness of soil may demand. Sharpen these so they can be easily driven into the ground as directed in paragraph 45 on "*Staking up.*" On one edge of these stakes drive wire nails—stiff six or eight pennies, having a large, flat head on them will answer. Drive the first nail near to top of each stake, and another each foot downward till the last rail would be about fifteen inches above the ground when set in the field, thus—

STAKE.

These nails should be set so as to incline upwards a little. See cut.

After your growing crop has been worked through thoroughly with the cultivator, then as described in paragraph 45, put in the stakes; only set these so that the edges, with the nails in them, will line along the row just over the plants. Set these stakes twelve feet apart in the row, or as near that as can be to set the stakes four inches from the plants.

WITH WIRE NETTING.

Buy in uncut rolls of one hundred and fifty feet each wire netting (such as is used for fencing poultry-runs or yards). It should be galvanized, having three

inch mesh, and such a width as will have it reach from
the lowest nail on the stake to the highest. Cut this
roll into twelve lengths, each twelve and a half feet long,
and hook on the nails on the stakes, stretching each as
tightly as a man can conveniently pull it, allowing the
ends to lap over each other on the nail in the stakes.
This affords a continuous trellis across the field. For
trellised tomatoes the ground should be marked, or furrowed out in three and a half, or four feet rows, running
north and south where at all convenient. The plants
should be set about two feet apart in the rows. In cultivating after the wire netting is put on the stakes use a
short single-tree, from a foot to fifteen inches long. To
the right end of it fasten firmly a piece of hickory, broad
enough to cover the end and clip on single-tree, and long
enough to reach eight inches up the tug. It should come
to a point at the upper end. When the tug is to be
hitched on that side, first slip on it a thin, flat iron ring,
then hook on the tug, and slip the ring down over the
point of the stick, until it is held firmly to the tug.

It may seem expensive to buy the wire netting; but
with care it will last for years, and is as cheap as anything else one can buy. To be sure, you can use other
kinds of wire fencing, such as the steel wire Fence Board
four inches wide; the Keystone; the McMullen; the

Sedgwick and the Page woven-wire fencing; or one can use smooth fence wires on each side of the stakes, running them the whole length of the row, a pair of them each foot upward from the ground.

The tying up and the pruning will be done the same as described for "staking up" (see paragraphs 45 and 46), except this: we suggest that about four shoots be tied up and spread out along the wires, so that the shoots will, as they grow up the trellis, be equal distances from each other. The particular advantage of the wire netting, or wire fence-board, or woven wire of any kind, is that no tying up is necessary; for when the grower pinches off unnecessary growths, he simply pushes the tops of the growing shoots, now *this way* and now *that way*, back and forth through the meshes, and they will retain their places so on to the top, when they may be cut off, or tied in a bunch above the trellis and left for a shade, if the season is hot and dry. If the grower has plenty of tall, slim undergrowth timber, he can cut long poles and nail these to the stakes; but then he must do some tying up for these. Attend to this fastening up and pruning every week in growing weather. It will take, at least, four prunings to "lay a crop by" in this thing.

You say this is too much work. Well, a great deal of it can be done in leisure times beforehand; and what can not, we can lessen a great deal by arranging to do it as conveniently as possible. Anyhow, a man must not growl about work, if he gets good pay for it. Try a few this way, and I venture you will soon see your way clear to put more out so. Tomatoes will be earlier, smoother, sweeter, cleaner, more easily harvested and marketed, bring a better price, and nearly as many more can be planted on an acre than for down-culture, and this saves fertilizers. The grower has, also, far better control over his crop, to work with it; to mulch, or to remove mulch-

FRAME TRELLIS.

ing, as the season is dry or wet; to apply spraying decoctions, or mixtures, against enemies; and to regulate sun and air to the fruits. It is justly growing in favor with advanced and careful market gardeners. It is an advantage, too, if one wishes a succession of crops, as early, medium, late—especially for the last named. Frost

will not cut them off so soon. Then, by removing the
late plants with a spade, when we reach the danger of
frosts, they will be in full bearing, and by rolling together
the twelve foot lengths of fencing, plants, roots and all,
they can, with care, be put on a sled, hauled to a shed,

HOOP TRELLIS.

unrolled and set up again to ripen after others are gone.
These will furnish fruits, quite fresh, till after holidays,
and bring good prices.

Tomatoes can be trellised on fences or on out-build-
ings, or on ornamental frame work of any kind as easily

as can a grape vine, and in the same ways and forms.
Only one thing remember, you must have rich soil, and
it must be thoroughly worked before you put the tomato·
vine into it; then water, trim and work well and you
will get elegant results. Some enrich two or three feet
square and two feet deep mixing in unleached ashes,
air-slaked lime and salt in the following proportions :
one bushel each of the ashes and lime, to ten pounds of
salt, and applying an inch and half of this mixture to
each plat, and work it well into a full spade's depth of
the soil. This will keep vermin of the soil out and act
as a fertilizer. On this plat is laid around the plant four
stout barrel-hoops of different diameter, then three or
four stakes are driven into the earth so that the hoops
can be nailed on or tied on them—the smallest at the
bottom, the next largest a foot higher and so on to the
top (see cut) only put two more hoops on than cut
gives. Shingling-lath or poles can be nailed into squares
or triangles or other shapes, and be employed as above
with the hoops. The tomato is to grow up and spread
out in these—trimming, tying up and cultivating as
before described in the paragraphs immediately preceding this one. This plan is for home use mainly or for
city-lot culture.

Trellis on Wire and Lath Combined.

On the authority of the Ohio Experiment Station,
I give the following plan for trellising, as it recommends
itself to my judgment, it is both cheap and practicable :
row them three and a half to four feet apart; trans-

plant in the rows two feet apart; set two strong posts
at the ends of each row, and brace carefully; set other
stakes between as may be needed, say every two rods;
take two wires, about the size used in baling hay, and
stretch tightly between these end posts, three and a half
feet from the ground; set now common plastering lath,
one to each plant, weaving the tops between the wires;
tie or tack up the plant to these, and trim as before ex-
plained. With care this is a neat trellis and staker
combined and will last for several years. It is also
cheap.

50. Tomato Culture under Glass.—I have visited thousands of hot houses in different parts of the
land and taken many notes of use from those who
manage them, which I am tempted to spread out upon
the pages of this book, but as my own personal experiences in this line are limited, I think it wiser for me,
and better for my readers to peruse an article prepared
by that well-known authority on this subject, Prof. E.
C. Green, of the Ohio Agricultural Experiment Station.
I give his article in full, because in addition to culture
under glass, he endorses in it many things already written in the preceding pages:

TOMATOES AS A SPRING AND SUMMER GREEN HOUSE CROP.

BY E. C. GREEN.

The prices that can be obtained for this crop in large quantities
in most of the western cities are not sufficient to pay for forcing in
midwinter. We have found, however, that the houses can be used to
good advantage in growing a tomato crop after the season for lettuce and other winter crops is over, and when the space is not
needed for anything else. Working with this object in view, we

use the house for other crops while the winter season lasts and keep
the tomato plants in as small a space as possible, which space is not
large enough to be seriously missed.   As a general rule, vegetable
houses are empty after the middle of May and produce nothing
after the lasts crops of radishes, and lettuce are taken off.   Vegetable houses could in this manner, with almost no cost for fuel and no
extra expense for filling benches with soil, be made to produce quite
an increase in income, the main work being the growing and training of the plants.

The demand for these house-grown tomatoes has been a constant surprise, and at no time have we had enough to meet it.   In
the midst of the strawberry and raspberry season tomatoes sold at
fifteen to twenty cents per quart, or about double the price of
berries.   Tomatoes were shipped in from the south, but did not
seem to hurt the sale of those from the greenhouse, being inferior in
quality and selling at lower prices.

In order to get plants ready to set in the beds about the middle
of March, or as soon as the second crop of lettuce is cut, the seed
should be sown about the middle of December.   If the seed is sown
much earlier than this the plants will become too large, and are liable to injury by crowding.   No special care is needed in germinating
the seed, but the young plants must have good care.   Tomato plants
are like corn in that they need all the warmth and sunlight they can
get, and at all times they should be kept in the warm part of the
greenhouse and not allowed to get chilled.   The soil should not be
allowed to get dry, but excessive watering should be avoided.   They
will thrive with less water than many other classes of plants.

After the plants get their second or third leaves they should be
transplanted, and at least once more before they are large enough to
be put where they will stand while fruiting.   When transplanted
the first time the plants are set 2x2 inches apart, and 4x4 the second
transplanting.   The plants may be set in beds or in pots, but for
various reasons flats are preferred.   These flats may be made of any
convenient size, but those in use here are 16x24 inches, and 2½
inches deep.   When the plants are set where they are to stand for
fruiting they are planted directly in the soil 18 or 20 inches apart
each way.   Large pots and boxes have been tried, but without any
apparent advantage, although this custom is recommended for forcing in winter.   Although sub-irrigation did not produce a marked

effect upon tomatoes, the beds where this system was in operation were watered with less trouble and more satisfactorily than those where surface watering was practiced.

The last transplanting should be done sometime in March, for after the middle of this month the benches cannot be used for lettuce profitably, as the houses are liable to get too warm, and the plentiful supply of hot-bed lettuce brings the price down ; but when the tomato plants are set out if good lettuce plants are set between them, a fair crop of lettuce may. be grown before the tomato plants reach any considerable size. But after the lettuce is off the tomatoes should have the entire ground, and should be given a good mulch of fine manure, which will assist in holding the water that is applied to the bed. After the lettuce is off, or perhaps before, the tomato plants should be trained to one or two stalks.

To train the plants some support must be given, and wire or string is preferable to stakes. The top of the wire may be made fast to the rafters, and the bottom anchored by means of sharp wooden pins of hard wood driven into the bottom of the benches, or by wire stretched across near the surface of the ground. The plants must be tied to these upright strings or wires frequently as they grow.

Pruning is another part of the work which is very important, not only to increase the size and earliness of the fruit, but to get the largest yield possible on the smallest space, and to keep the plants in good shape. It is not the nature of the tomato plant to confine itself to a single stalk, and when compelled to do so its efforts to grow side branches are very persistent. Not only will sprouts come out at the axil of each leaf, but the ends of the blossom stalks will develop into branches and even the upper surface of the main vein' of the leaves will throw out sprouts. All of these must be taken off, or there will be a tangled mass of vines if the plants are very close together.

VARIETIES.

"The varieties that do well out of doors are the ones that will do well in the house. It is best to raise the kinds that the market demands. The Acme and Beauty are the best of the purple kinds that have been

tested, although no better than some of the red sorts.
Among the red kinds the Perfection and Paragon are
good. The Lorillard, which has been highly recommended for forcing, has not done as well under our system as some others. The early, rough varieties are not
desirable, as the pruning seems to make them more irregular. We have given the Atlantic Prize, one of the
best of this class, a thorough trial, and have discarded
it because it does not sell well. The same remarks apply with even greater force to Hundred Day, King of
Earlies and Salzer's Earliest of All. The Dwarf Champion has some qualities to recommend it. The plants
can be set closer together and nearer to the glass than
other varieties. The first fruits that set are of fair
size, while on some other varieties they are small. It is
difficult to prune on account of the heavy leaves hiding
the sprouts, and it does not yield heavily. The Golden
Queen is one of the best of the yellow kinds, but there
is little call for a yellow tomato in this season of the
year. The Potato Leaf is the opposite of the Dwarf
Champion as regards ease in pruning, as it grows very
long and spindling. It does not yield heavily, but the
fruit is quite shapely and of fair size.

"Besides the kinds mentioned, we have tried
Ignotum, Matchless, Michel's New, Livingston's Stone,
but they have no qualities that render them more desirable than those first named. Bulletin 28, June, 1891,
Cornell University Experiment Station, by Prof. L. H.
Bailey, touches many points in tomato forcing not
treated of in this paper, and will be found useful to
those wishing to force tomatoes in mid-winter."

Prof. Green thus advises tomatoes as a spring and summer crop under glass after lettuce and other product. It can then be forced with profit. He says: "The essentials to be regarded are, (*a*) to have the plants sufficiently advanced to set in the beds about the middle of March, or as soon as the last crop of lettuce is cleared off; (*b*) to prune off all the lower branches and suckers; (*c*) to keep the plants tied up to supports."

51. Tomato Enemies, Diseases and Remedies.
—It is encouraging to know, that as a field crop the tomato has fewer and less formidable pests than any other crop of so extensive culture.

But it has some, and every grower will get acqainted with them (often to his sorrow), as the crop passes through its various stages from sewing the seed to the ripening of the fruit. We will mention some of them under their common names, together with such remedies as are good to use.

52. "Damping Off."
—I name this first, because you are likely, as a grower, to meet with it first. It is a trouble that manifests itself while the plants are young, by rotting them off near the surface of the ground. You will observe them to bend over, wither away, and die. There is difference of opinion as to the cause of it; but I favor the idea that cold, dark, damp weather encourages it. If there is added to it an atmosphere that is foul to the tomato, such as one might

expect to find in a hot-bed unventilated or not aired out daily, one would expect to find such a result. If this is the cause, then the cure is better ventilation, more judicious heating, and greater dryness.

53. Cut-Worms.—If you plant on sod-ground, or on an old pasture, plowed up (which is very good for a tomato crop), then look out for cut-worms. Your plants will not be long in the ground until you will see that something has cut them off near the ground. Sometimes these are very destructive, just as they are on corn. I consider it an advantage to plow late in the fall, and it will not hurt to plow again in the spring. Tearing up the ground thus often, seems to destroy the worms, and generally upsets their designs upon a tomato crop.

If it is remembered that the plants are set out in the field quite a considerable distance apart; and that this worm does not eat off roots only by accident, but comes out at night to feed on the stalk, and that it burrows into the ground again when his meal is over, leaving the traces on the surface, where he went into it; then it will not seem such an insuperable task to go and hunt them out and kill them. They are rarely more than an inch down in the soil. A few hours' work will kill many, and save many a plant. Robins, yellow hammers, meadow-larks, bluejays, mocking birds, and quails, are very fond of these worms, and are generally friends of the grower. I encourage all laws that defend them, even if they do feed on our cherries be-

times. Sometimes I think they take these more for
the worm in them than for the cherry. Toads should
also be let alone in your fields, for they do no harm, but
keep fat on such pests as cut-worms. I know they are
not particularly handsome creatures, yet upon more inti-
mate acquaintance with the toad, we are reminded of
the old and true adage, "Pretty is that pretty does."
Besides he has ways—real cute ways—of disposing of
these worms; you only need to see him do it once to
be ever after his friend. I know of nothing that can
be put on the plant to kill these worms which will not
also injure the plant. Slug-shot, stirred pretty liberally
and thoroughly into the ground around the plant to the
depth of an inch, will kill the worms, and act to some
extent as a fertilizer for the plant.

54. Colorado Potato Bugs.—We all know this
bunchy beetle and how destructive his ravages are. We
all know how he "does business on the first floor," em-
ploying his whole family, from the least even to the
oldest. Seems like they do all possible to push on the
work of destruction to its bitter end. But it does not
relish the tomato as it does the potato, and so is not
so bad on it, yet it does attack the tomato and do harm
sometimes. Take an old fruit-can and punch holes into
the bottom with a nail, or better with a round long
punch from the inside outward, fill with slug-shot or
other insecticide and dust the plants thoroughly while
the dew is on them. It will then stick to them, kill the
bugs, also cause the everlasting slugs to loosen their

grip and bite the dust in the agonies of death. They can be treated in the same ways as are common when on potatoes.

55. The Tobacco-Worm.—It is a large green worm, about three and a half inches long, and three-eighths of an inch in diameter. It has a long horn upon his rear back, and when disturbed he jerks himself from side to side, and twists himself about as though he meant to do dangerous work with this horn, but it is like the feints of a drone-bee to sting,—it don't do any hurt. When tobacco was a great crop in these parts it was called the " tobacco-worm," but it is known mainly as the " tomato-worm " now. It feeds on leaves and green tomatoes mainly. During this last year—1892— it was the most formidable enemy that ever attacked the tomato in these regions. The first thing to do is to raise a good sized bed of petunias near the tomato field, so as to have them in full bloom by the time the tomato plants are growing nicely in the field. If you are about these petunia beds in the early evening, you will soon discover a large miller—almost as large as a humming bird—attracted by the sweet-scented flowers. He is in search of honey. If you watch him closely as he hovers over a flower, you will see him unroll a long proboscis, two to three inches long and kept in a most beautiful coil under his nose when not in use, thrust it into the flowers and take up the sweets that are hid away in its depth. Now while he eats thus is your opportunity, having a short, broad paddle in hand slap one on the other with said

miller between them, or hit her a clip with one paddle
hard enough to kill a rat, for this dusty and lusty insect
is the moth that lays the eggs which will hatch out in
due time into the tomato-worm. Therefore visit the
petunia beds each evening, and make the destruction as
thorough as possible, for each one you destroy keeps
many worms from appearing on the crops later. Two
careful, spry boys or girls will, with a small reward for
each dozen millers they kill, thin them out wondrously.
But if the worms do appear upon the plants, as effectual
a method for destroying them as any, is to put a thin,
tough switch in the hands of the abovesaid boys or girls
and direct them to give each one they see a quick, smart
stroke which will cut them in two and destroy them.
Reward them at so much a dozen and offer a slight
premium for the one who gets the greatest number
killed. Their sharp eyes, nimble feet and agile hands
will not fail to reach most of them with their switches
and sever their connection with the tomato business
forever.

Nature usually provides to keep matters on a
balance by raising one thing to feed on another. But
man in his ignorance and folly interferes with these
wise arrangements, and often destroys this balance.
This I always think of when I see different parts of
birds on ladies' hats, knowing that with the over-killing
of birds will come the over-production of insects. Now,
in regard to the destruction of this worm the grower
has a formidable ally in a long-legged ground-colored
fly. It covers the worm with small, white eggs or nits

about one-sixteenth of an inch in length. This fly
stands high on her legs a few inches behind the worm
while it is eating, and enjoying its repast so well that it
is at peace with all the world, and suspects nothing;
then quick as the bot-fly, it darts forward and fastens
the egg on the flesh of the worm. Of course it makes
heroic efforts to stab the fly to death with its bold-look-
ing horn, while the fly stands back in place unharmed,
and apparently enjoying its safety, and success, and the
prospect of another deposit soon. As soon as the
worm forgets his sorrows, and, acting from the impulses
of a voracious appetite, begins to eat again, the alert
fly deposits another live egg upon its carcass. And so
it keeps on until it sometimes literally covers the worm
with eggs, which soon suck the life out of the worm,
and it works tomatoes no more for a living. This is
more important than many suppose, viz., not to kill
these flys, nor destroy the worms which have the white
eggs on them, for I have good reasons to believe that
the flys usually deposits its eggs upon the female worms,
and rapidly destroys the source of supply for lusty
millers, and one-horned hungry worms. It is never
mean assistance to get the help of the allies of nature
in the destruction of the pests which prey on our
growing crops.

56. Tomato Blight.—Of this I have had no experience, but I see it mentioned in scientific writings
about the tomato. I will give a quotation or two, giving their [remedies, for this may prove helpful to my
readers in some part of the country:

A Remedy For A Tomato Pest.

I inclose a tomato twig. You will help many by publishing the cause and remedy of its trouble, as it is next to impossible to raise tomatoes on this account. The vines are attacked in all stages of growth until the fruit is full grown. If a plant ripens its fruit without any sign of the trouble, it is not attacked.—[G. W. Wilgus, Takima county, W. T.

The plant sent to me is affected by a little fungus known to botanists as Cladosporium fulvum. This little parasite grows in the tissues of the tomato and destroys all the parts with which it comes in contact. It is propogated by means of minute bodies called spores. As a means of preventing it, I would suggest that the plants be sprayed, every two weeks during the growing season, with a solution made by dissolving half an ounce of flour of sulphur to the gallon of water. The first application of this solution should be made before the disease appears, or when it is first noticed. The effect of the treatment is to prevent the spores from infecting the growing vines, and to do this care should be taken to reach all these parts with the spray.—[Prof. B. T. Galloway, United States Department of Agriculture.

Mr. J. W. Day, of Central, Miss., in his book, says: "This disease is spreading very fast in the South where tomatoes are often grown in the same locality. It begins by the vine becoming wilted for a day or two, then the bottom leaves turn black and slough off. Sometimes the leaves turn yellow the first two or three days."

"The best preventive is to change patches every year, as they are dead-sure to be affected with blight if you do not let the land rest a year or two between crops. There is some fungus in the vines, and rotting tomatoes left lying about, that literally impregnates the land with this disease, and blight will surely appear the next year. It is worse on a dry year than a wet one. It is often kept over on the stakes. These ought to be fumigated, or disinfected. Take crude carbolic acid,

one part acid to twenty parts water, and sprinkle the
stakes or trellising to be used again well with this
mixture."

Another thing I would at least guess to be an
advantage, and that would be to gather up all affected
or decaying vines or tomatoes and burn them, and to
keep this work done up as closely as possible without
destroying good vines or fruit. If any fungus disease
appears in culture under glass, everything must be
cleared out, the whole place disinfected, new soil, new
plants and new supports found for them; and to do this
too, every fall. Again I would think judicious spraying would do good. Hope our Experimental Stations
will tell us soon about it. It might be too, that fertilizers could be found such as potash lime and salt mixture which would destroy the fungus that causes this
blight. By all means let us have some thorough experiments on it by our Southern growers and Experiment
Station men.

57. Black Rot in Tomatoes.—This, as its name
indicates, is a disease that appears first at the blossom
end of tomatoes, and is worst upon the earliest kinds.
Later in season it usually disappears. Coming on the
earliest it becomes the dread of Southern growers and
all who aim for " earlies." The cause of it is not certainly known, and I sincerely hope some ambitious
experimenter will make himself justly renowned by
learning and telling us all about this trouble.

One writer says : " Sufficient critical attention has
not been given to this question, yet there appears to be
some truth in the idea that fresh stable manures tend to
induce this fungus disease, hence chemical manures are
to be preferred for this crop."

We give also the experience of another as follows :

WHAT CAUSES TOMATO ROT?

G. H. MAHAN, CHENANGO CO., N. Y.

It is variously claimed that this disastrous disease is the result of
either extremes in temperature, an exceedingly wet or dry season,
the using of plants grown from seed saved from a previously affected
crop, etc. Now, while I would not say that these causes may not
tend to this effect, yet I am inclined to the belief, based on experience, to attribute it more directly to the fact that the plants had
suffered a sudden check at some period of their growth.

Each spring I raise large quantities of garden and bedding
plants, Tomatoes being one of the principal ones of the former. After
being transplanted once or twice in the boxes or " flats " in which
they are grown I usually set them in the open ground quite closely
together, removing them from there as wanted for selling. I usually
try and leave a plant every three or four feet in the row to mature
its fruit.

The foregoing is what was done the past season, and now the
point I am trying to make is this: plants were taken from this bed
and removed to three different locations in towns widely separate,
combining at least two very different soils, and in each instance
three-fourths of the fruit borne on these vines were affected with rot
at the blossom end, while the plants left remaining in the rows bore
exceedingly fine fruit, perfectly free from the affection. Now why
was it ?

Certainly the season was the same in each case and they were
all from the same seed. To my mind it was clearly the cause given
above ; that at the time they were taken from the bed and set out,
the weather being very dry, the plants sustained a check in their
growth which so weakened their vitality that they became an easy

prey to their most common ailment. Care should therefore be exercised at all times in setting such plants to arrange to do so in a wet or cloudy time and thereby remove the tendency to this fatal disease.

It is also said to be worse in a dry season. Now the causes would sum up about this way : Stunting the plants by either extremes of cold or heat, too great change of temperature in transplanting, viz : from warm, moist hot-beds to dry, cool frames, or to open field, when cool and dry and without sufficient moisture at the time, and possibly fungus growths produced by too much fresh manures in the soil about the plants. The cure for this last would be to use chemical manures or at least well-rotted manures with which has been mixed hard-wood ashes, lime and salt.

The preventives for the others is best possible preparation of the soil by deep plowing, thorough pulverizing, judicious fertilizing and watching better the conditions of heat and cold, and more care when transplanting. I submit also the opinions of others on "*staking up*" as a means of preventing rot :

TOMATOES ON STAKES IN WET WEATHER.

I notice that N. S. complains of his tomatoes rotting badly on the ground. I have not for many years been troubled in that way, as I have trained them to a single stake, and by pinching off three to five of the lower shoots and afterwards tying the leader firmly to the stake, the fruit is kept up and grown perfect. The stake needs to be a good one, about six or seven feet long, firmly driven into the ground. Of course, there is some work in this manner of growing the crop, but it has the advantage of growing a fourth to a third more plants, getting the weeds out of the way easily, and having more and finer fruit.—G. N. S., *Wellesley Hill, Mass., in the American Garden.*

TOMATOES TRAINED TO STAKES.

Last spring I concluded to give the Perfection Tomato a fair trial on stakes. I had a garden in the heart of the city 150x180 feet, surrounded by a fence six feet high. On the sides facing east, west and south I set on May 25th, three hundred plants that had been well grown, and five-inch oak stakes six feet long by one-and-a-half inches square were driven into the ground beside each plant. The plant was allowed to grow but one stem, all side shoots being pinched off until the top of the stake was reached. They require the pinching and tying four times during the season and set an average of six clusters of tomatoes. Not one rotted and the flavor was so superior that we had as ready sale for them for slicing as we found for our strawberries, and at from ten to twenty cents per quart when bushels were offered in the groceries at from twenty-five to sixty cents per bushel. The first ripe tomatoes were picked July 21, and the last on Nov. 4th. For retail sales or family use I shall never train in any other way.

Steubenville, O.

The advantages of staking, or trellissing, become more and more apparent each year, and in each direction we may think of it. If the Black Rot is caused by any fungus growth, "staking up" will permit of spraying to advantage against it. Always destroy all tomatoes and vines on which Rot appears.

58. "The Borer."—This is a short, stout worm that buries itself into the body of the fruit. It is the same as you see sometimes in sweet corn, inside the husk, and imbedded into the very kernel itself. This pest is worse in the South as it appears also among the cotton. It is moving northward, however, and is already showing symptoms of becoming an enemy to be feared by tomato growers. Its early destruction should be sought for by all diligently.

Friend Day suggests to kill the moth at night by open lights in the field, into which they fly, and are killed; to spray with weak decoction of London purple, or sprinkle it dry on them, but only a very little in a place, as it burns the leaves of the tomatoes; and to plant sweet corn along side of the tomato field, as they prefer it above a tomato diet. They will gather on it and leave the tomatoes almost entirely alone. He also suggests to gather all tomatoes which show signs of cracking, or evidences that the worm is in them, because it will bore into several tomatoes before it quits. These should be, when gathered, mercilessly destroyed.

A few years experience will teach the grower much about these pests and diseases. Let me suggest that you watch constantly and carefully whatever endangers your success. Remember, everything in this world has its drawbacks; and every crop has its difficulties that beset it. The man succeeds best who learns as he goes on to lessen these more and more and to add to his business little advantages which increase his income. It only takes a few such leverages over your competitors to turn the trade your way. Watch for them and work for them. It pays.

59. Harvesting, Marketing, Shipping and Selling.—As these items of business occur together, we will describe together. The tomato is perishable fruit and must be disposed of within ten days after they begin to ripen. To put it in round numbers, ripe fruit may begin to appear in one hundred days after seed is put into the ground. Many conditions of season, culture and soil enter in to vary this time for "earliest of all" however, and you must remember that in building up your expectation. I see some seedsmen advertise kinds that will ripen in seventy-five days after sowing the seed. While I do not discourage your trying a packet, I feel much safer in directing you to be ready to harvest in one hundred days, or even later. Whenever it does come, you must be ready to do quick work. Get reports and keep posted on the markets. Have all boxes, crates, baskets and hands to use them, at command, for even a day's time will lose, or make you money as you use it.

60. Harvesting, etc., for Shippers.—Remember this is a time when you will be in a hurry. As one grower said to me, "It will be dollars to you often to get them into market quickly." Long before the crop ripens then use up some leisure moments in securing four good, stiff peck-baskets for each picker you are to employ. Line them with felt paper or similar soft material and cover with muslin. This is to keep the rough parts of the basket from bruising the fruit as it is picked into them. You cannot be too particular about keeping the fruit whole. It is always money to you to get your fruit into market in the best possible condition, and this means the most scrupulous care from first to last in handling it.

Have ready four-quart and eight-quart boxes, also three-peck and four-peck crates, such as are ordinarily used for shipping. Of course if you can invent something better and that will sell your fruit better, do not hesitate to use it.

It will be necessary if you handle any great acreage, to have a packing shed which should be roomy, light, dry and as handy as you can arrange everything to do the work well and quickly.

For the first picking, each gatherer takes two of the lined peck-baskets, goes into the field and picks only those which are full-grown and all that show the least tinge of red at the blossom ends.

Put only the most careful hands at this work.   If you must work some careless fellows, let them carry to the packing house and return with other empty baskets for the careful pickers.   Direct these to push off the stems and anything else that may be on them ; to *place* them—not throw or drop them, even for an inch—into the baskets.   There must be no *bruises* made in picking or getting ready for market or there will be *black* places when unpacked to sell, and this means either lower price or none at all.

When the baskets are full, *carry*, not *haul*, to the packing house ; and this suggests that it may be advisable to locate it centrally in your field.   In no case pour out of the baskets, but pick out with the hands ; wipe off the dirt and sort into lots to suit your crop to the trade. Mr. Day, of Mississippi, has had about as much experience as anyone else, and he advises to divide " into seven grades—ripes, mediums and greens, and each of these again into two grades, viz., into large ripes and small ripes; large, medium ripes and small, medium ripes; large greens and small greens, while the culls make the seventh grade and are not to be shipped at all." As Mr. Day says of the above grading, they look better, sell better, keep better and pack better.

If he who sorts them in the packing house arranges a set of six flat trays—one for each assortment—on some support about him at a convenient height, that is, in front of him, two trays, two on the right and two on the left hand, then by placing the full basket from the field between him and the middle tray so that the top of it will be even with the top of the trays, he can clean and sort into the trays rapidly and accurately, just as he removes them from the basket. He should be careful not to mix colors in same trays. When dry, they are packed into the boxes and crates, hurried away to the cars to fly by day and by night away to the Northern markets.

When packed they should be marked on outside of crates just what they are, and in due time commission men and other salesmen will learn your brand and seek your stock. They can make more out of them and will give more for them. That the reader may know how commission men feel about this business, I will quote from Mr. P. M. Kiely's " Southern Fruit and Vegetable Shippers' Guide and Manual:

"The importance of proper handling, packing, etc., is not properly estimated. If ripe Tomatoes are going to be gathered, be sure you put them in a separate box; but ripe stock should not be sent forward unless you are only a few hours' ride from market. Even then they are liable to arrive in bad order.

Generally speaking, the proper time to gather and pack is when
the tomato is full grown and beginning to color or partly colored,
depending upon the time of transit. The warm weather prevailing
at the time will ripen them fast enough. You should not lose sight
of the fact that a good many are wanted for re-shipment, and to be
fit for this trade, the best we have must not be fully ripe when they
reach us. When shipped by freight they must be gathered still
sooner, when full grown, before coloring sets in. Freight is not desirable unless you have some assurance in regard to time. A good
many come from the South by freight that are almost worthless on
arrival. Last year considerable came entirely too green; that is,
were picked and shipped before *full grown*, and most of such stock
arrived rotten. The regular peach box (one-third bushel) should
be used.

The best packing usually appearing in this market (St. Louis)
is that from Southern Illinois, where the most experienced growers
reside. Their packing is almost perfect. No knotty, stunted, over-
ripe, or otherwise imperfect stock should be put in the box under
any circumstances. The receipts from that section are always sought
by the shippers here in consequence. There is a very wide demand
for the Tomato; all classes being purchasers as soon as the price
becomes reasonable. The demand for it is steadily on the increase.

A great deal of money has been made off the Tomato, not only
in the South, but also North and East. The South is destined, however, to remain the most profitable region to cultivate them for commercial purposes. The improved facilities and lower rates for
reaching Northern or distant markets, continue to afford substantial
encouragement. An acre of ground can be made to yield enormous-
ly in efficient hands; from one hundred to four hundred bushels,
according to circumstances, location, etc. Two hundred is, perhaps,
the limit in the South, and four hundred in the North.

As to varieties, will say that the "Acme" should head the list
for this market, and for most other markets, too, as it is a universal
favorite. Livingston's "Beauty" and "Perfection" close to it, and
any smooth, round, medium-sized variety might be added."

Sometimes they are wrapped like oranges in paper.
I see almost none upon the northern markets in that
style, I merely mention it here in passing. It should be

used for the first picking anyhow and also for the most fancy markets in the largest cities. It can be done to advantage for this kind of a market.

61. Harvesting, etc., for Short-Distance Shippers.

—I refer to those not over twenty-four hours away from northern cities; they might be called intermediate shippers. They need not harvest and ship until the fruit is riper. They will reach the markets in good shape and out-sell all the earliest varieties that come farther to market. These come in between those grown in the extreme south and the "first early" of the north, and certainly meet a good demand, but to get this trade the intermediate shipper must exercise great care in picking, packing and getting them promptly on the market. Pack tomatoes for this market at such a degree of ripeness that they will reach the market ripe. Place them tightly in the crate, so as to leave none loose, but do not mash them. Remove the stems and wipe each tomato with a cloth as they are put in. Make a special effort to have only the choicest fruit go to market. It may not seem to pay you, but persevere until you get your name up in some market for always having choice products, and then your success is assured. Not as much is made of this trade as might be by growers. Go to Southern Illinois and take some lessons.

62. Harvesting, etc., for the Home Market Gardeners.

—This is done, not for the fun of it, but for the money there is in it. This means, put up your stock

or fruit in the best possible condition to be attractive
and desirable by those that use them. I am aware that
my readers are liable to get tired being *told* this thing
so often, but I am also aware that the home market-
gardener must not get tired *doing* this or he will suffer
loss. The matter of first importance to him is to get
ripe tomatoes a few days earlier, if possible, than most
other people. If you can do this, you get the *first run*
on tomatoes and impress it on the minds of all classes of
customers, that you are "well-up" in the business, are
a careful man and expect to serve them well. To encourage you in this, remember that most of the work
you do to get this result, will come before spring or
summer work commences, when, in all probability you
would not do much else anyhow, but it is just that much
ahead of the ordinary time of working, that only a few
will *take the trouble then*, to do what is necessary to have
ripe tomatoes for the home market during the last days
of June or the first of July, see paragraphs from 45 to
51, for the culture necessary to attain this end.

You will need the same preparations for your crop
as are given in the last two paragraphs and such other
as we may name as we go along. Gather these first-
ripe, home-grown tomatoes into felt-lined baskets and
handle them like eggs, with care. *Carry* them to the
house and sort as before described, only into four grades,
viz. : ripes and nearly ripes, and these again into larger
and smaller. Always cull out those which would hurt
sales. Never put an inferior article on the market, it
will pay you far better to throw it away entirely, although

any kinds of tomatoes are relished by hogs, cattle or poultry and if given in small feeds will do them good. The " earliest of all" should be put in berry-boxes and sold at the same price as strawberries. Of course, these will be mostly grown under glass; but raise a few this way because it lets you in ahead of others and gets the trade. The second " earlies" are to be assorted into one-quart and four-quart boxes or baskets. These should always be rounded up well in the box, so as to look as full as possible, not to look like they would roll off. They should all be "faced up" in the boxes from the bottom to the top; that is, put the tomatoes in the box with the blossom ends up, or all the stem ends down. Some people say this is not honest, but these same persons would curry a horse well if they were taking it off for sale. It seems to me perfectly legitimate to make our fruit as inviting as possible. Every young lady acts on this principle, and rightly too, for you and I, my dear friend, would not want to make a wife of a slouchy girl. But see to it that you do not put the nicest ones on top and the poorest in the bottom. That is a misrepresentation and is not honest, nor will it pay. While it is right to make the most and best of what we have, it is not right to sell inferior for good and people will not be duped by us long in this or any other way. Sell in the one-quart boxes as long as you possibly can, for there are thirty-two of them in a bushel, and at a few cents a quart you are getting a better price per bushel, than if you sold at bushel rates. You can do this too, because many only want enough at this time of year for

slicing for one day's use, and do not mind a nickle or
even a dime for a box of choice ones. Have some real
ripe and some only half-ripe from which to fill up the
box. It pays to suit the customer's taste. Get them to
market as early as possible ; but do not try to com-
pete with the fruit away down South, as that would be
useless. But my early tomatoes are picked fruit, and
have a very different appearance and flavor from that of
the South and I usually get very fair prices. As they
get cheaper you can put in an extra one now and then,
as it may be appreciated, but you must not spoil your
customers by being too free with donations.

Never empty a box or basket into a customer's
market-basket ; always lift them out with the hands and
" face them up " as they were in your own basket, then
they will look as they are and also appear to be what
he bought of you. It takes a little time, but if you say
something a little cheery while you do it you will
satisfy your customer and that goes a good ways in
bringing him back to you again. Whether you sell
from the wagon, or on the street from the table, aim to
appear at regular times and as near in a given place as
possible. The customers will look for you and wait till
you come. This is the time to take orders for canning.
There will likely be some very nice cracked ones among
your fruit, especially during some seasons. Never put
these in with the rest, but put in a lot by themselves
and " lump them off " to some one who wishes bulk
rather than quality and with a little reduction on regular prices, you can turn them off and get all they are

worth. After this, as you approach to the bulk of the crop, gather into boxes or crates, which you ought to make yourself, so that they will fit your wagon and not jostle about in it, for this spoils tomatoes for canning. Also they should hold exactly, when rounding full, a peck, a half bushel and a bushel. Take these directly to the field and as you pick, rub off stems and dirt, sort into the crates and as fast as full, place in the wagon. This saves handling, but does all necessary at once, and if picked and packed thus, when the weather is dry or nearly so, they will get to market in excellent shape. You can't gather so fast this way, but you can get all done that ought to be done this way as fast as any and handle them but once. Of course, do not forget to "face up" as already described. Observe the same rule about not turning them in the baskets or upon a customer's table. Talk nicely all the while, "face them up" in a nice neat pile upon the kitchen table and you will please this time and sell more readily at another time. Don't forget that a measure only level full will not sell one-half as quickly as one rounding full.

The bulk of the crop is sold for canning, and if you are fixed to handle a large quantity there is a handsome profit in it at thirty-five cents a bushel. When the height comes I go to the canning houses and get a fair price, carrying them the very best quality and all uniform in appearance throughout. I have found that in whatever you are dealing and no matter with whom, if your fruit or vegetables are just as fair and large at the bottom and middle of the package as at the top, the price will be better than in any other way. Persons who are accustomed to buying know at once how to rate their customers. Five cents or ten cents on a bushel makes a large sum in the aggregate, and will pay the buyer as well as the seller, if he knows at a glance what he is getting and can depend upon it. Start a wagon out over your city, and supply the poor with cheap, wholesome tomatoes, and still get a fair price for it at this time.

As for late ones it pays well to aim to meet this demand. Some people never get anything done when it ought to be done, and so they will not get their tomatoes canned till the bulk of crop is harvested and sold; if now one has nice fruit to sell then he can do so at a good figure. It will pay to risk hitting this market. It is not a question of "can I sell them?" but "can I have them?" See paragraph 49 for methods of culture, so as to get them with reasonable certainty and safety.

One should keep favorably acquainted with commission men and the markets in different places, and often shipments can be made to advantage. On the advantage of late crops and sales I quote from the "Maryland Farmer," as follows:

"I raise a bed of tomato plants in the open ground for late planting. They are pretty fair sized plants about the first of June, and a quarter of acre in the field is reserved for them. They come forward generally fully as well in proportion as the early plants. I have one pretty good picking from them of ripe fruit; but as frost approaches they are usually loaded with good-sized green tomatoes. I have sold some of these green tomatoes, but I do not give that as much attention as I might, for I have something better in view.

"I have a good warm cellar of large dimensions, and across this I stretch poles, just as for hanging tobacco, and I pull up the tomato vines by the roots, loaded as they are with green fruit, and hang them, tobacco fashion, on these poles in the cellar.

"There they gradually ripen from the beginning of frost to the Christmas holidays, and when I go to town with my little stock and get my 25c or 30c or 35c a quarter of a peck for them, it pays.

"If I had a big cellar, properly prepared for the work, I could coin more money from an acre of late tomatoes, with less actual expenditure of labor, than from any other crop that is grown in the vegetable line.

"I give my brother farmers this item, trusting it will do them as much good as it has done me. I remember the first time I carried in a few bushels of these tomatoes, expecting a little spare change from them, and came back with $19.45 for them, I felt a great deal astonished at what I had done. But it has got to be a common thing now and I give it to you."

63. The Uses of the Tomato.—I claim to be a "ladies' man" in the best uses of that phrase; and I want to put something in my book for them. The uses of the tomato enters now into the daily food of nearly every family, in the city or in the country. It is both a vegetable and a fruit; and has uses co-extensive with all vegetables and all fruits. I know of no other one garden or field crop that can be put to so many varied uses as the tomato, and still be so palatable to most appetites.

It may be canned for home use, or general markets, as other fruits. It makes soups by itself, or with anything else used in this way. It makes excellent sauces, salads, catsups; or pickles, sweet, spiced, and sour, green, ripe, or in mangoes. They can be sliced, baked, escalloped, dried, fried, made into figs, stewed, or into anything else desired; and it is a wholesome diet for sick or well; old or young; rich or poor; leisurely or laboring; wise or otherwise; saint or sinner.

I here append some recipes, not for reading as much as for reference and to show the various and principal uses of the tomato. I do this with becoming modesty; for a man feels about as awkward telling the ladies how to cook, as a woman would feel were she to attempt to plow a straight furrow across a forty-rod field. I ought to say, too, that I have gleaned these recipes from all kinds of sources, but have submitted them to the judgment of competent cooks who declare them valuable and reliable. Use, if possible, only fresh, nice tomatoes, and you will be apt to get them if you secure as soon as they get cheap enough for you to invest in the quantity you wish to use. The last of the season are never so good as the first; and especially after frosts have hurt the vines.

Tomatoes for the Sick.—"The tomato is the best of all vegetables as an article of diet in sickness, especially in bilious diseases. I have heard that they contain calomel, or the properties of it, and was, therefore a medicine as well as an article of diet. When one is first beginning to recover from a bilious attack they can eat a tomato with a little salt on it when they can take nothing else, and if you don't like tomatoes try to learn to eat them, for it is a most useful taste to cultivate. I think it was the hardest task I ever set myself to learn to like them, but I was determined I would learn, and I did, and most sincerely thankful have I been since, particularly when recovering from an attack of chills and fever."

Mother's Sliced Tomatoes.—"Prepare half an hour before dinner, scald a few at a time in boiling water, peel, slice, and sprinkle with salt and pepper, set away in a cool place, or lay a piece of ice upon them. Serve as a relish for dinner in their own liquor. Those who desire may add vinegar and sugar."

Sliced Tomatoes.—"Scald ripe tomatoes; let them stand in cold water fifteen minutes. Then take off the skin and slice in a dish garnished with sweet peppers."

It adds to the above to employ tomatoes of differant colors and serve in alternate layers, also choose those of about the same size, or otherwise put the largest layers in the bottom of the dish.

Sliced tomatoes may be served with Mayonnaise salad-dressing which is made as follows: "Into the yolk of one raw egg stir all the olive oil it will hold; if dropped in very slowly, half a pint of oil can be used; season with cayenne pepper, salt and mustard."

Raw Tomatoes.—Peel and slice with a sharp knife. (Tomatoes should always be cut just before using.) Lay in salad bowl and season with dressing, made in following proportions: Beat together four table-spoons vinegar, one teaspoon each of salt and sugar, half as much mustard, and when these are well mixed, add gradually two tablespoons of best salad oil.

Stewed Tomatoes.—"Scald by pouring boiling water over them, peel, slice and cut out all defective parts; place a lump of butter in a hot skillet, put in tomatoes, season with salt and pepper. Keep up a brisk fire and cook quick as possible, stirring with a spoon or chopping up with a knife (in the latter case wipe the knife as often as used or it will blacken the tomatoes.) Cook half an hour. Serve at once in a deep dish lined with toast. When iron is used, tomatoes must cook rapidly and have constant attention. If prepared in tin or porcelain, they do not require the same care."—MRS. JUDGE COLE.

Fried Tomatoes.—No. 1. "Slice tomatoes quite thick; pepper and salt them; roll in flour; and fry in equal parts of butter and lard. Put them in a dish to be served and keep hot. A little flour and butter mixed; stir into the skillet with a cup of milk; boil until well thickened; pour over the tomatoes."

No. 2. "Same as above, only after rolling the layers in flour dip them into beaten egg, then fry, etc. These may be served with or without the flour, butter and milk dressing named in No. 1."

Tomato Toast.—"Run a quart of stewed ripe tomatoes through the colander; place in a porcelain stew-pan; season with butter, pepper, salt and sugar to taste; cut thin slices of bread, brown on both sides, butter and lay on a platter, and just as the bell rings for tea add a pint of good sweet cream to the stewed tomatoes, and pour over the toast."—MRS. S. WATSON, Upper Sandusky.

Tomato Custard.—"This is recommended in the Modern Cook Book as a good diet for invalids. Make a custard of four eggs, one quart of milk and one cup-ful of sugar; add one pint of stewed tomatoes, and bake quickly in small cups."

Escalloped Tomatoes.—No. 1. "Put in a buttered baking dish a layer of bread or cracker crumbs, seasoned with bits of butter, then a layer of sliced tomatoes seasoned with pepper, salt and sugar, if desired, then a layer of crumbs, and so on till the dish is full, finishing with the crumbs. Bake from three-quarters of an hour to an hour. Onions, prepared by soaking over night in hot water, dried well, and sliced in nearly half inch slices, and browned on both sides in a frying-pan with butter, may be added, a layer on each layer of tomatoes."

No. 2. "Put alternate layers of sliced tomatoes and bread crumbs into a bread-pan; season with sliced onion, butter, pepper and salt; bake for one hour."

Baked Tomatoes.—No. 1. "Cut a thin slice from blossom side of twelve solid, smooth, ripe tomatoes; with teaspoon remove pulp without breaking shell; take a small, solid head of cabbage and one onion; chop fine; add bread crumbs rubbed fine and pulp of tomatoes; season with pepper, salt and sugar; add a teacup of good sweet cream; mix well together; fill tomatoes, put the slice back in its place, lay the stem-end down in a buttered baking dish with *just enough* water (some cook without water), with a small lump of butter on each, to keep from burning, and bake half an hour, or until thoroughly done; place a bit of butter on each, and serve in baking dish. They make a handsome dish for the dinner table."—Mrs. S. Watson, Upper Sandusky.

No. 2. "Fill a deep pan with ripe tomatoes (as many as will lie on the bottom), after first rounding a hole in the center of each and filling it up with bread crumbs

or crushed crackers, and seasoned with butter, salt, pepper and sugar; Pour a teaspoonful of water in the pan,
to prevent from burning.   Bake brown, and send to the
table hot."

Broiled Tomatoes.—"Take smooth, flat tomatoes;
wipe, and set on gridiron, with stem-end down, over
live coals.   When this is brown, turn them over and let
cook until quite hot through; place them on a hot dish;
dress, when eaten, with butter, pepper and salt."

Tomato Soups.—No. 1. "Take a quart of canned
tomatoes, add a pint of hot water, and when all boils
add two spoonfuls of flour, mixed smooth with a little
cold water.   Stir until it boils again, add an onion
chopped fine, then let it cook for twenty minutes, stirring occasionally.   Strain through a sieve, add a gener-
ous piece of butter, salt and pepper to taste, and a tablespoonful of sugar."

No. 2. "One quart of tomatoes, one quart of milk,
one quart of water.   Boil the water and tomatoes together about twenty minutes, and then add the milk;
then one teaspoonful of soda.   Let it just boil up.   Season as you do oyster soup, with butter, pepper and salt;
add crackers if desired."—Mrs. Simon Gerhart.

No. 3. "Meatless Tomato Soup: One quart tomatoes,
one quart water; stew till soft; add teaspoon soda; allow
to effervesce, and add one quart boiling milk; salt, pepper and butter to taste, with a little rolled cracker; boil
a few minutes, and serve hot."—Mrs. D. C. Conkey,
Minneapolis, Minn.

No. 4. "Skim and strain one gallon of stock made from nice fresh beef; take three quarts tomatoes, remove skin, and cut out hard center" [none is in my varieties]; "put through a fine sieve, and add to the stock; make a paste of butter and flour, and, when the stock begins to boil, stir in half a teacup, taking care not to have it lumpy; boil twenty minutes, seasoning with pepper and salt to suit taste. Two quarts canned tomatoes will answer."—MRS. COL. REID, Delaware, Ohio.

No. 5. "Maccaroni with Tomatoes: Take three pints beef soup, clear, and put one pound maccaroni in it; boil fifteen minutes, with a little salt, then take up the maccaroni, which should have absorbed nearly all the liquid, and put it on a flat plate and sprinkle grated cheese over it thickly, and pour over all plentifully a sauce made of tomatoes, well boiled, strained, and seasoned with salt and pepper."

Tomato Pie.—No. 1. Southern Tomato Pie—"For one pie, peel and slice green tomatoes; add four tablespoons vinegar, one of butter, three of sugar; flavor with nutmeg or cinnamon; bake with two crusts slowly. This tastes very much like green apple pie."—MRS. CEBA HULL.

No. 2. Mutton Pie and Tomatoes—"Spread the bottom of a baking dish with bread crumbs, and fill with alternate layers of cold roast mutton, cut in thin slices, and tomatoes peeled and sliced; season each layer with pepper, salt and butter. The last layer should be tomatoes spread with bread crumbs. Bake three-quarters of an hour, and serve immediately."

No. 3. Beef Pie and Tomatoes—"Scald the tomatoes; skin and quarter them, and sprinkle with salt and
pepper. Bury the meat in a stew-pan with tomatoes;
add bits of butter rolled in flour, a little sugar, and an
onion minced fine; let cook until the meat is done and
the tomatoes dissolved into a pulp."

Ham with Tomato.—"When you are tired of cold,
boiled ham, try cooking it this way: Cut the ham in
rather thick slices; put in your stew-pan one can of tomatoes which have been run through a colander; add a
little chopped onion and celery; stew half an hour; rub
a tablespoonful of flour into one of butter; add this to
your sauce; season to taste; let it boil up, then put in
the ham and cook five minutes."

Tomato Preserves.—No. 1. Preserved Tomatoes—
"Take one lemon and one pound of light brown sugar,
to one pound of tomatoes. Grate the thin yellow rind
of the lemon, then pare off the thick white part which
is not to be used, slice it thinly, and remove all the seeds.
Scald, and peel the tomatoes. Put water enough with
the sugar to dissolve it, and when it is boiling remove
the scum and add the tomatoes. Cook slowly for two
hours."

No. 2. Green Tomato Preserve—"To one pound of
fruit use three-quarters of a pound of granulated sugar.
Allow one sliced lemon to two pounds of fruit, first
tasting the white of the lemon to be sure it is not bitter.
If bitter, use the yellow rind, grated, or shaved thin,
and the juice. Put the sugar on with just water enough
to melt it, add the tomato and lemon, and cook gently

until the tomato is tender and transparent. Cut the to-matos around in halves, and then quarter the halves. This shape is preferable to slices. This will keep with-out sealing, but it is better to put it in small jars, as it is so rich that only a little is wanted at a time."

No. 3. "Scald and peel carefully small, perfectly formed tomatoes, not too ripe (Yellow Pear or Plum-shaped and Gold Ball are the best), prick with a needle to prevent bursting, add an equal amount of sugar by weight, let lie over night, then pour off all juice into a preserving kettle and boil until it is a thick syrup, clari-fying with white of an egg, add tomatoes and boil care-fully until they look transparent. A piece or two of root ginger or one lemon sliced thin to a pound of fruit and cooked with the fruit may be added."

No. 4. Tomato Figs.—"Allow half a pound of cof-fee-sugar to every pound of tomatoes. The yellow plum tomatoes, or the very small and perfectly smooth red ones are preferred for this method of preserving. Put the sugar on the stove with just water enough to melt it. As soon as it boils, put the tomatoes in whole with the skins on. Draw the kettle back where they will simmer gently. Cook until transparent, about two hours. Skim them out carefully, and drain off all the syrup. Spread them on platters to dry, in the sun, if possible. Sprinkle a little sugar over them while dry-ing, and the next day turn them, and sprinkle again with sugar. Do so for two or three days. When suffi-ciently dry, pack in boxes. Seven pounds of tomatoes will make two quarts of figs."

No. 5. " Tomato Jam.—Take one-half pound of
sugar to one pound of tomatoes, put together in a stone
jar and let stand twenty-four hours, then take off the
juice and strain it; put it into a porcelain kettle, bring
to a boil and skim; then put in the tomatoes with a
handful of stick cinnamon tied in a cloth; stir all the
time. About ten minutes before removing from the
fire, take out the cinnamon and add one teacupful of
good vinegar to one gallon of jam. Boil until the jelly
will not separate."

No. 6. Tomato Butter.—Among all the "butters"
so famous on the old-fashoned farm tables, we fancy
tomato butter scarcely found a place. A Pennsylvania
housewife recommends it. For a trial mess, "take two
and a half quarts of tomatoes and three quarts of apples.
Stew separately until smooth, mix well, and add three
pounds of sugar, one tablespoonful of cloves and twice
as much cinnamon. Boil until thick enough to suit the
taste."

Canned Tomatoes.—"These are merely stewed tomatoes sealed in cans while hot. Some points to remember are that freshness is necessary; that overripeness is
a fatal defect, and that the later tomatoes are never so
good as those which ripen earlier."

A bushel of our kinds will put up fourteen to eighteen cans, while our mothers used to get only eight to
ten cans from a bushel of the best sorts, and usually
about half of these would spoil in consequence of a
green core. It makes a great difference whether or
not you have kinds to can that are smooth, solid and
which ripen early. See paragraph 28 for kinds.

No. 1. " Tomatoes should be canned in August, when the fruit is in the best condition. It is highly important that the fruit should be perfectly sound and not too ripe, for a single spot of decay will contain a sufficient number of ferment-germs to spoil the entire mass.

" These are the most reliable methods :

"Have a large kettle of rapidly-boiling water on the stove. Wipe the tomatoes, fill a wire basket with them and plunge it into the boiling water until the skins begin to crack. Then plunge into cold water, and remove the skins and the hard part under the stem.

" Mash thoroughly and let them boil quickly until perfectly soft, but not enough to evaporate all the liquid. Then season as for the table. To every quart, allow one teaspoonful of salt, one salt-spoonful of pepper and half a cup of sugar. Cook five minutes longer, then fill the jars almost full. Have ready some butter, melted, strained and boiling hot, in the the proportion of one tablespoonful to every jar. Fill to the brim with the hot butter and seal at once. Olive oil may be used instead of butter. Wrap the jars in paper and keep in a dark place. Examine the jars after two weeks, and if any of them show signs of ferment, turn out the contents and treat as directed in making catsup, which see."

No. 2. " Prepare as in the first recipe, but season only with salt. Let them boil down until quite thick, then fill the jars nearly full, add boiling water to the brim and seal at once. Be careful that no seeds or pulp run over the edge between the glass and the rubber. Keep the jars wrapped in paper, in a cool place. Use these only for soups and sauces."

No. 3. "The tomatoes must be entirely fresh and not over ripe; pour over them boiling water, let stand a few minutes, drain off, remove the skins, slice crosswise into a stone jar, cutting out all the hard or defective portions. (If my varieties are used, no need of this.) Cook for a few minutes in their own juice, skimming off the skum which rises and stirring with a wooden spoon or paddle; have the cans on the hearth filled with hot water, empty and fill with hot tomatoes, wipe moisture from top with soft cloth, put on and secure covers.

"If tin cans are used, press down covers and pour hot sealing wax in grooves. If put up in glass, put away in a dark place. Either tin, glass or stone cans may be used and sealed with putty instead of sealing wax, it being more convenient."

No. 4. Canned Corn and Tomatoes.—"Scald peel and slice tomatoes (not too ripe) in the proportion of one-third corn to two-thirds tomatoes, put on in porcelain kettle, let boil fifteen minutes and can immediately in glass or tin. (If glass, keep in the dark.) Some take equal parts of corn and tomatoes, preparing same as above, others after cutting corn from the cob, cook it twenty minutes, adding a little water and stirring often; then prepare the tomatoes as above, cooking in a separate kettle five minutes and then adding them to the corn in the proportion of one-third corn to two-thirds tomatoes, mixing well until they boil up once and then can immediately.—MRS. D. BUXTON.

Tomato Pickles.—No. 1. Ripe Tomato Cold Pickle—
"Sixteen medium-sized ripe tomatoes, four small green
peppers, four small onions, all chopped fine. Then add
one cup of vinegar, one cup of sugar, and half a cup of
salt. Mix thoroughly, and put up cold."

No. 2. Uncooked Tomato Pickle—"Cut one peck
of green tomatoes in quarter-inch slices, sprinkle over
them one cup of salt, and let them stand twenty-four
hours. Then drain very dry. Slice twelve small onions
thin. Mix one small bottle of prepared mustard, two
tablespoonfuls of ground cloves, one tablespoonful of
ground pepper, and one of allspice. Then into the jar
in which the pickle is to be kept, put alternate layers of
tomato, spice and onions, until all is packed. Cover
with cold vinegar, and let them stand until the tomato
looks quite clear, when they are ready for use."

No. 3. Green Tomato Pickle—"Chop enough green
tomatoes to make a gallon, sprinkle over them half a cup
of salt, and the next morning drain and squeeze dry.
Add one teaspoonful each of cinnamon, cloves, whole
mustard seed and celery seed. Pour on vinegar enough
to cover, and boil twenty minutes."

No. 4. Whole Tomatoes for Winter Use—"Fill a
large stone jar with ripe and perfectly sound, whole
tomatoes, adding a few cloves and a sprinkling of sugar
between each layer. Cover well with one-half cold vinegar and one-half water. Place a piece of thick flannel
over the jar, letting it fall well down into the vinegar,
then tie down with a cover of brown paper. These will
keep all winter, and are not harmed even if the flanne
collects mould."

No. 5. Ripe Tomato Pickles—"Pare ripe, sound tomatoes (do not scald); put in a jar. Scald spices (tied in a bag) in vinegar, and pour while hot over them. This recipe is best for persons who prefer raw tomatoes."

No. 6. Ripe Tomato Pickle—"Pare and weigh ripe tomatoes, and put into jars and just cover with vinegar. After standing three days pour off the vinegar and add five pounds coffee sugar to every seven pounds of fruit. Spice to taste, and pour over tomatoes, and cook slowly all day on back of stove. Use cinnamon, mace and a little cloves, or not any, as preferred."

No. 7. French Tomato Pickles—"One peck green tomatoes sliced, six large onions sliced; mix these and throw over them one teacup of salt, and let them stand over night. Next day drain thoroughly, and boil in one quart of vinegar, mixed with two quarts of water, for fifteen or twenty minutes. Then take four quarts vinegar, two pounds brown sugar, half pound white mustard seed, two tablespoons ground allspice, and the same of cinnamon, cloves, ginger and ground mustard. Throw all together and boil fifteen minutes."—MRS. PRESIDENT R. B. HAYES.

No. 8. Green Tomato Pickle—"Take eight pounds green tomato and chop fine, add four pounds brown sugar and boil three hours; add a quart vinegar, a teaspoonful each of mace, cinnamon and cloves and boil about fifteen minutes, let cool and put into jars or other vessels. Try this recipe once, and you will try it again."—MRS. W. A. CROFFET, New York City.

No. 9. Piccalilli—"One peck of green tomatoes and one head of cabbage chopped fine; mix with them one large cup of salt, put all into a coarse cheese-cloth bag, and let it hang and drain over night. Then chop six large onions and four green peppers, mix them with the tomatoes and cabbage, pour over them enough hot, weak vinegar to cover and drain again. The next morning scald the same amount of good sharp vinegar, and pour over them, add two tablespoonfuls of whole mustard-seed, and when cold it is ready to use."

No. 10. Piccalilli — One peck green tomatoes, sliced; one-half peck onions, sliced; one cauliflower, one peck small cucumbers; leave in salt and water twenty-four hours; then put in kettle with handful scraped horse-radish, one ounce tumeric, one ounce cloves (whole), one-fourth pound pepper (whole), one ounce cassia buds or cinnamon, one pound white mustard seed, one pound English mustard. Place in kettle in layers, and cover with vinegar. Boil fifteen minutes, constantly stirring."

No. 11. Sweet or Spiced Tomato Pickles—" Four quarts cider vinegar, five pounds sugar, one-fourth pound cinnamon, two ounces cloves to seven pounds of fruit." (Think about half-ripe tomatoes will give best satisfaction here). "Scald the vinegar and pour over the fruit. Pour off and scald vinegar twice more at intervals of three days, and then cover all close. A less expensive way: Take four pounds sugar to eight of fruit, two ounces cinnamon, one ounce cloves, one teaspoonful salt, one teaspoonful of allspice."

Tomato Catsups.—No. 1. " One peck of ripe tomatoes, four large onions sliced, three-fourths of a cup of
salt, three tablespoonfuls of black pepper, one tablespoonful of red pepper, one tablespoonful of allspice,
half a tablespoonful of cloves. Mix all together, and
stew them until very soft, about two hours. Just before taking from the fire, add one quart of vinegar, and
rub through a colander. Put on to boil again, then
seal at once."

No. 2. " Stew the tomatoes until soft, then to
every gallon of stewed tomatoes add one-fourth of a
pound of salt, one-fourth of an ounce each, of red pepper, pimento, and garlic, one-half of an ounce of ginger-
root and of cloves. Stew all together until reduced
enough to pour easily, then strain into bottles, and seal
with wax."

No. 3. Cold Catsup—" Peel and chop fine half a
peck of ripe, sound tomatoes. Grate two roots of
horse-radish, and chop fine one cup of onions. Mix all
well, and add one cup of salt. Bruise half a cup each,
of black and white mustard seed in a mortar, and mix
with them two teaspoonfuls of black and one of red
pepper, one tablespoonful each, of mace and cinnamon,
and two teaspoonfuls of cloves, one cup of sugar, and
one quart of vinegar. Mix all these ingredients very
thoroughly, and put it into jars."

No. 4. Tomato Catsup—" One peck of ripe tomatoes, cut up, boil tender and sift through wire sieve;
add one large tablespoonful ground cloves, one large
tablespoonful allspice, one large tablespoonful cinnamon,

one teaspoonful cayenne pepper, one-fourth pound salt, one-fourth pound mustard, one pint vinegar. Boil gently three hours. Bottle and seal while warm."

No. 5. Tomato Catsup—"One gallon tomatoes (strained), 6 tablespoonfuls salt, three tablespoonfuls black pepper, one tablespoonful cloves, two tablespoonfuls cinnamon, two tablespoonfuls allspice, one and one-half pint vinegar; boil down one-half. One peck tomatoes will make one gallon strained."

No. 6. Tomato Soy—"One-half peck tomatoes, one large pepper cut fine, one large onion cut in slices, one tablespoonful each of ground allspice, black pepper and celery seed, one-fourth cup of salt, one-half pint of vinegar. Boil all together slowly one hour; cool, and bottle for use."

No. 7. Green Tomato Catsup.—"One peck green tomatoes, one dozen large onions, one-half pint salt; slice tomatoes and onions. To layer of these add layer of salt; let stand twenty-four hours, then drain. Add one-fourth pound mustard seed, three desertspoons sweet oil, one ounce allspice, one ounce cloves, one ounce ground mustard, one ounce ground ginger, two tablespoonfuls black pepper, two teaspoonfuls celery seed, one-fourth pound brown sugar. Put all in preserving pan, cover with vinegar and boil two hours.

No. 8. "Half bushel tomatoes, four ounces salt, three ounces green peppers, one ounce cinnamon, one-half ounce ground cloves, one drachm cayenne pepper, one gallon vinegar. Slice the tomatoes and stew in their own liquor until soft, and rub through a sieve fine enough to retain seeds and boil the pulp down to the consistency of apple butter (very thick), stirring steadily all the time to prevent burning; then add the vinegar and a small teacup of sugar and the spices, boil up twice, remove from the stove and let cool to bottle. Those who like onions, may add a half dozen medium sized ones peeled and sliced about fifteen minutes before the vinegar and spices are put in."—Mrs. M. M. Munsell, Delaware, O.

No. 9. " Take one bushel fine, ripe tomatoes, wipe them off nicely and put in porcelain kettle. Place over fire and pour over them about three pints water, throw into it two large handfuls of peach leaves with ten or twelve onions, or shallots cut fine; boil till tomatoes are done, or for two hours; then strain through a course mesh sieve, pour the liquid back again into the boiling kettle and add one-half gallon good cider vinegar, have ready two ounces ground spice, same ground pepper, same mustard, whole; one ounce cloves, two grated nutmegs, two pounds light-brown sugar, one pint of salt; mix well together, put in kettle and boil two hours, stirring continually to prevent scorching. If it is desired to "hot," add cayenne pepper to your taste. When cool, fill bottles, cork tightly, seal with wax, keep in a dry, cool place."—G. D., Baltimore, Md.

No. 10. " Take one gallon of strained tomatoes, four tablespoonfuls of salt, one and a half of allspice, three of mustard, eight pods of red pepper; grind the articles fine, simmer slowly in strong vinegar three or four hours, then strain through a hair sieve, and bottle.

Enough vinegar should be used to have half a gallon of liquor when the process is over."

No. 11. " Cut up ripe tomatoes, boil soft and strain ; put them on again and boil half down; then to every three and a half gallons of juice, put twelve tablespoonfuls of salt, six of pepper, one of allspice, one of mustard, one of mace, one-half of cloves, one of ginger, six small pods of red pepper chopped fine; boil hard one hour."

No. 12. " To one and a half bushel of tomatoes use the following spices : Three ounces of cloves, two of allspice, a little cayenne pepper and plenty of black pepper and salt, and a pint of vinegar to each gallon ; tie up a few onions in a bag and boil with the catsup; boil half down."

No. 13. " One-half peck of Tomatoes, run through a sieve; one teacupful of salt, one of mustard seed, six red peppers, three tablespoonfuls of peppers, one-half gallon of vinegar, piece of horse-radish, one teacupful of nasturtions, half a cup of celery seed. Do not cook, but seal tight in bottles."

No. 14. Tomato-Mustard—" Take one peck of tomatoes, cut them into a porcelain kettle, boil until soft, rub through a sieve, put the pulp back in the kettle, and boil until quite thick ; take one teaspoonful of cayenne pepper, one of white, half a one of cloves, two of mustard, one tablespoonful of salt. Let all boil together a few minutes, then stir in half a pint of vinegar. When cool, bottle and cork tightly."

Tomato Salad.—" Take the skin, seeds and juice from nice, fresh tomatoes, chop what remains with celery and add any good palatable dressing."

Tomato Sauce.—No. 1. " Place on fire, tomatoes washed clean, broth, onion, parsley and seasonings; boil to a pulp—about thirty-five minutes; rub through fine sieve, return to fire, stir in butter, and serve."

No. 2. " Pare, slice and stew tomatoes for twenty minutes, strain and rub through a sieve; put into saucepan with a little minced onion, parsley, pepper, salt and sugar. Bring to a boil, stir in a good spoonful of butter rolled in floor; boil up and serve."

No. 3. " Stew ten tomatoes with three cloves and salt and pepper for fifteen minutes (some add a sliced onion and sprig of parsley), strain through a sieve, put on a stove in a sauce-pan in which a lump of butter the size of an egg, and level tablespoonful of flour have been well mixed and cooked; stir all until smooth, and serve. Canned tomatoes may be used as a substitute."

No. 4. " For green tomato sauce, cut up two gallons of green tomatoes, take three gills black mustard seed, three tablespoons dry mustard, two and a half of black pepper, one and a half of allspice, four of salt, two of celery seed, one quart each of chopped onions and sugar, and two and a half quarts good vinegar, a little red pepper to taste."

Tomato Omelette.—" Skin two or three tomatoes, cut in slices, fry in butter, beat up some eggs to make omelette, season with salt and pepper, warm some butter in pan, put in the eggs, stirring well to keep from adhering, mix in tomatoes, turn out omelette on plate, doubling it in two. Another nice way is to roll up tomatoes in omelette and serve with tomato-sauce."

There is one thing all tomato-eaters should remember, that the flavor of a tomato is very delicate. It escapes readily with much handling, shaking, knocking or hauling about. Get it and consume it when it comes as directly from the vine as possible. Let market-gardeners also catch the hint. Hurry to the kitchens of your customers with as much care and celerity as you can. They will taste all the better, and so increase the demand for your productions. I do not believe, that the full use to which tomatoes can be put, has as yet been attained. I sincerely ask all expert or amateur cooks, who have a good way of using them, to send us the recipes for same, and it will find a place in our next edition. I heartily commend such to try other methods of using tomatoes, as may be suggested to them; and, if they prove valuable, let us know about it.

64. The Extent of Tomato Culture.—My readers will be impressed with the greatness of the business about which I have written, by statements like the following: "It ranks next in importance to that of Irish potatoes. It is well for us to know the best methods of cultivation, so as to produce the greatest quantity, with best quality, and *when* we need them *most*." I hope this book will meet that felt necessity to a reasonable degree. "A single county in Maryland has over $1,000,000 invested in the canning business."

"The people of Cobden, Ill., are particularly proud of their tomato crop, and on this popular vegetable the town 'does herself big.' She has been known to ship thirty-three carloads of tomatoes in one day, and this does not include several carloads hauled over to Mountain Glen, a town on the Mobile & Ohio Railroad, and within a few hours after this great train load was sent off, at least fifty carloads more could have been picked."

From the Virginia Experimental Station, as follows: "Few are aware how important the cultivation of special crops is now becoming in Virginia. In all the Eastern States, in fact, the tendency of agriculture is in the direction of specialties, and the tiller of the soil who would not fall behind in the race must recognize this fact. As one among such special crops, the culture of tomatoes holds a high rank. Statistics sufficient to give definite information in reqard to the money value of this crop in Virginia have not yet been collected by the Station. Judging, however, from general statements, there must be in this State no less than *eighty*, and probably as many as *one hundred*, canneries working on this crop, either alone or in conjunction with other fruits. In addition to this, the market crop grown in the vicinity of Norfolk and on the Eastern Shore, will reach about one-half the value of that used in the canneries. Hence, it seems fair to say that the value of the tomato crop grown for these two purposes alone—for the canneries and for market—cannot fall short of *one million dollars* annually. This takes no account of what is grown in a general way for local markets and home consumption. As already stated, the estimation is not based upon an accurate knowledge of facts, but there is every reason to believe that it is within bounds."

Prof. W. H. Bishop, Horticulturist of the Maryland Experimental Station, has the following to say of the business in that State: "To-day the tomato may be classed as one of the most important garden vegetables, and, in fact, its culture has so far extended beyond the limits of the garden that it is rather a field crop than a garden crop. In Maryland alone there are not less than twelve thousand acres yearly devoted to growing this crop, and only about one-fourth of the acreage of the country is found in this State. There are two hundred packing houses in this State that devote the whole or part of the season to canning tomatoes. The prominence and magnitude of this industry have induced us at the Maryland Experiment Station to give special attention to the questions affecting the grower and packer."

The growing of tomatoes is fast spreading into newer countries for the older countries to consume, as the following clip from a recent number of the "American Agriculturist" will show: "Efforts are being made to establish a trade for South African tomatoes and potatoes in London. Tomatoes would be needed in the London market during January, February and March, and potatoes during February, March and April, and it is urged that the latter be grown in red soil where possible. The London vegetable dealers are prepared to pay from one and one-half to two cents per pound for tomatoes, which would pay the farmers, one of whom guarantees to supply from eighty to one hundred tons of the Acme and Perfection varieties." It also shows what kinds are reaching from American soil to London markets, and then from "the survival of the fittest" there, finding its way into "Darkest Africa."

I now quote in full from the "American Grocer" of New York, January 11, 1893. This need not be read, but is placed here for reference, to show what the business was when this volume was written:

TOMATO PACK—1892.

" We take pleasure in presenting our thirteenth annual report of the pack of tomatoes throughout the United States and Canada. The total output is slightly behind that of 1891, the shortage amounting to 38,673. It appears, however, that the total output is above the average of the past six years and slightly behind that of the past three years. It is apparent that the present consumptive requirements of the country are beyond the average annual pack for six years of 3,179,214 cases. It is certain that the total output of 1892 will have passed into consumption long before another season's operations have commenced. Had it not been for the very favorable weather toward the close of the season, throughout New Jersey, the shortage would have been much larger. In the West there was a great falling off in the output. Wherever a shortage occurred, it was due to unfavorable climatic conditions.

" We separate the report of Canada from our usual tables this year because that market is practically closed to the United States. The pack in Canada this season was comparatively heavy. Tomatoes are selling in Canadian cities at 75 cents per dozen. Were it not for the duty of 45 per cent. they might be available for use in the United States. Here is an instance of the wisdom of the McKinley tariff in protecting American canners against the competition of Canadian packers.

" Throughout the season there has been an unsatisfied demand for high grade goods. It is gratifying to note that there is a steadily widening market for fine brands and that consumers evidence a willingness to pay for quality, even if some jobbers are reluctant to discriminate between standards and extra, to the extent packers deem remunerative for the extra expense their packing involves. There has been a difference of from 10 to 25 cents per dozen between the price of brands, due wholly to variations in quality and the estimation put upon brands by the retail trade and consumers. Established labels that have represented high and uniform quality command full prices.

" As usual our statement is based on actual returns received from packers and commission merchants, to all of whom we return thanks for their prompt answers and willingness to institute special inquiries. The following table, the pack of 1892, in comparison with that of 1891."

PACK BY STATES.	1892.	1891.
New Jersey	862,692	950,833
Maryland	977,742	744,010
Indiana	282,717	341,217
California	230,943	218,311
Delaware	175,700	264,950
New York	146,290	114,774
Virginia and West Virginia (2000)	60,386	98,360
Iowa	57,500	94,800
Ohio	87,840	90,590
Missouri	64,621	90,350
Michigan	39,602	73,506
Illinois	42,200	68,324
Kansas	30,833	50,700
Utah	55,000	.....
Nebraska	2,210	26,900
Pennsylvania	18,950	15,000
Connecticut	14,750	14,400
Colorado	39,262	12,600
Massachusetts	6,557	10,000
Kentucky	2,200	10,000
Arkansas	2,500	14,500
Tennessee	.....	6,840
Texas	100	4,500
North Carolina	1,5 0	3,900
South Carolina	7,500	.....
Alabama	1,170	.....
Georgia	12,400	3,000
Total United States	3,223,165	3,322,365
Canada	143,627	83,000
Total United States and Canada	3,366,792	3,405,365

"The above table represents the minimum number of cases packed. Many new factories have been started in the Southern States and some of them have not reported. The total output in 1892 compares with the pack of previous years as follows:

	CASES OF TWO DOZEN TINS EACH.
1892	3,366,792
1891	3,405,365
1890	3,166,177
1889	2,976,765
1888	3,343,137
1887	2,817,048
Total for six years	19,075,284
Average per year	3,179,214
Average per years 1890-1892	3,312,778

" Since our last we have chronicled the death of
Mr. Harrison W. Crosby, to whom belongs the credit of
first introducing canned tomatoes, packed in tin cans,
as an article of trade. He lived to see the industry
expand from an experimental point until it was located
in nearly every State in the Union. Mr. Crosby's first
pack was put up in 1848, while he was a steward at
Lafayette College, Easton, Pa. A common iron sink
was used as a bath. What great advantages have been
made in the application of steam and machinery,
whereby the cost has been reduced from 50 cents per
can, at which prices they sold in 1848, to an average of
7 cents per can for the past seven years! Demand has
increased and the supply expanded, while the cost has
steadily declined."

MARKET REVIEW.

"The year opened with confidence in the market.
Although the pack of 1891 was the largest for years, it
was not beyond the requirements of the country. It
was apparent early in the year that there would be no
carry over, as in the days gone by, when new season's
goods were met by tomatoes anywhere from one to four
years old. The Western Packers' Association held
about 80,000 cases at the beginning of the year. In
March the trade began making contracts at 87½ cents
delivered for New Jersey brands. April was a quiet
month so far as sales for future delivery were concerned;
the spot market was inclined to easier figures.

"In May there was renewed demand for contracts. Early in the month a favorite New Jersey pack was sold at 85 cents, delivered here. Harford County No. 3 offered at 75 cents per dozen net cash f. o. b., and No. 2 tins at 57½ cents. San Francisco reported sales for future delivery at 75 cents, less 1½ per cent. for No. 3 tins. In June offerings were light, but prices did not advance. Sales on contract were freely made at 75@77½@80 cents f. o. b. Harford County. During the summer spot stock continued scarce and high. In July New Jersey brands sold at 87½ cents and Delaware brands at 85 cents for forward delivery. San Francisco quoted 80@82½ cents. Some fears were expressed at this time as to the crop, there being too much rain and too many bugs. Late in the month the market for futures was 2½ cents higher. Spot stock also improved, so that 90 cents was obtained in Baltimore and 92½@95 cents in New York. August opened with free sales of futures at 87½@90 cents for New Jersey brands; 82½@85 cents for Harford County.

"Deliveries of 1892 tomatoes commenced about the middle of August, causing a drop in quotations for spot. The quality of the first shipment was not of a high order. Reports during August were not favorable for a large pack, particularly in the Western States. Drouth caused an active demand to spring up, brokers reporting heavy sales in early September, chiefly from the West. Sales were made at 80 cents cash, f. o. b. Harford County, for large blocks. The market was firm throughout the month, with light offerings, as dry weather continued and fears were expressed for the result in the Atlantic Coast States.

"Toward the close of September and early in October, the weather in New Jersey, Delaware and Maryland was very favorable for tomato vines, the canneries running full time and some working nights. This weather continued for some time, so that the estimated shortage in the pack was overcome. The market continued to rule in packers' favor, as it was apparent that the total supply was to be behind that of the previous year. Ninety to ninety-two and a half cents was readily paid in New York for No. 3 standard, while 85 cents cash f. o. b. was the lowest price in Harford County. In November some of the heaviest operators in the country reported their stocks the smallest held at that time for several years. The demand continued good until the close of the year. Prices ruled in sellers' favor and closed firm at one dollar, at which price sales were made.

"The following range of prices for the year in New York, Philadelphia and Baltimore will convey an idea of the condition governing the market throughout the year. The figures represent prices for good standard No. 3 tins, and generally represent grades of that quality and not such as are regarded extra."

"The following table gives the range of prices for each month in the year for standard No. 3 Tomatoes in New York, Philadelphia and Baltimore:

	N. Y. & N. J. No. 3.	PHILADELPHIA.	BALTIMORE.
January	$0 85 @ 90	$0 75 @ 77½	$0 75 @ 80
February	82½ @ 90	77½ @ 80	80 @ 82½
March	85 @ 90	80 @ 82½	80 @ 82½
April	82½ @ 87½	80 @ 82½	80 @ —
May	82½ @ 85	80 @ 82½	80 @ —
June	85 @ 87½	82½ @ 85	82½ @ 85
July	87½ @ 92½	82½ @ 85	85 @ 90
August	90 @ 92½	85 @ 87½	85 @ —
September	90 @ 95	77½ @ 80	82½ @ 90
October	90 @ 92½	82½ @ 85	87½ @ 90
November	90 @ 92½	85 @ 87½	90 @ —
December	92½ @ 1 00	87½ @ 90	90 @ 1 00

"The following table gives the highest and lowest prices for standard grade of Tomatoes in No. 3 tins in the New York market for seven years:

Highest and Lowest.

1892	$0 82½ @ 1 00
1891	80 @ 85
1890	77½ @ 1 00
1889	82½ @ 88
1888	90 @ 1 05
1887	95 @ 1 10
1886	88½ @ 1 15

"The following table brings into comparison the price of No. 3 standard Tomatoes in Philadelphia on January 1, each year for the past nineteen years:

Jan. 1—		Jan. 1—	
1893	95	1883	1 00
1892	75@80	1882	1 22
1891	75@80	1881	1 10
1890	75	1880	1 20
1889	92½	1879	90
1888	97½	1878	1 90
1887	90	1877	1 70
1886	90	1876	1 50
1885	75	1875	1 30
1884	80		

NEW JERSEY.

"New Jersey loses its place as the banner State, Maryland taking that honor. The output in 1892 was 862,692 cases, falling off from the preceding year 88,141 cases. The season opened about a week later than in 1891. Most of the houses opened between Aug. 20 and Aug. 25, while some did not commence operations until early in September. The packing closed at most places between Oct. 15 and Oct. 25. The first setting of fruit was marketed in good shape, but the second setting was injured by dry weather, and for a time fears were entertained for the pack, but late in the season climatic conditions were exceedingly favorable; so much so that the expected shortage was reduced to the small quantity noted above. Messrs. Kirby Bros. and Mrs. Sarah Aldrich, of Burlington; Messrs. Brown & Dunn, of Trenton; the Diamond Packing Co., and West Jersey Packing Co., of Bridgeton; Chamberlain & Co., of Mercer County, are among those who discontinued work during the year. Among the new factories was the Hopewell Valley Canning Co. at Hopewell."

DELAWARE.

"Delaware falls behind last year 89,250 cases on account of drouth. In some sections of the State the pack was very light, about one-half that of previous years. The factories opened between Aug. 20 and the first of September, and closed between Oct. 15 and 27. The old firm of Calhoun and Thoroughbred was termi-

nated by the purchase of Mr. Thoroughbred's interest
by Geo. C. Calhoun. Their factory is located at Georgetown. J. N. Maxwell operated the factory formerly
run by Carsins & Maxwell. The factory of A. W. Small,
at Lincoln, was operated by Thomas U. Marvell. Among
the factories discontinued were Macklin & Co., at
Georgetown, Thomas Dutton, at Redden and one at
Shelbyville."

NEW YORK.

"The packing in this State did not begin until
about the first of September, although one or two
houses started operations a few days earlier, and some
not until the middle of September. The pack terminated early owing to frost. Many houses packed none.
The New York State Preserving Company, at Buffalo,
was discontinued. The factory at Fairport, formerly
operated by C. & H. J. Burlingham, was operated by
Howard Thomas.."

MARYLAND.

"There were quite a number of factories discontinued in Harford County, during the past year, while
we have added a few names. The packing opened early,
some houses getting at work during the first week in
August. The season terminated at various dates in
October, some houses not closing until nearly the end
of the month. Some of the packers report a yield of
400 bushels of fine Tomatoes per acre. One of the
packers writes that he finds it very profitable to sow
seed as early as February, and to get strong plants out

about the first of May. He is of the opinion that the
early grown fruit is far superior to the late crop. Taken
altogether, the season in Harford county must be considered a good one.   Had it not been for drouth the
pack in Harford county would have been heavier. In
some sections the yield was cut down one-half by dry
weather. The pack of the city of Baltimore was ahead
of last year. It reached a total of 373,000 cases. We
do not count in the Baltimore estimate, Tomatoes packed out of the city, but carrying the label of Baltimore
packers."

CALIFORNIA AND UTAH.

"The season opened about the first of September and
closed the latter end of October. One house reports not
having closed until the first of December. Utah figures
in our table for the first time. Three factories in the
Territory report an out-put of 55,000 cases."

INDIANA.

"The season in this State opened early in August
and terminated during the last half of September.
There were a number of new factories in the State, one
each located at Seymour, Ewing, North Indianapolis,
Knightstown, Monticello and Spiceland. Several factories in this State packed an average of 30,000 cases each."

ILLINOIS.

"The pack in Illinois was 26,124 cases behind that
of last year. The season opened late—not until the
last part of August, and closed during the last fortnight
of October. The crop was poor.

IOWA.

" This State falls behind last year 37,300 cases. The season opened toward the end of August and continued until the latter part of October. The factory of The Potter Canning Company was removed from La Motte to Wyoming. The factory at Fairfield was discontinued."

MISSOURI.

" Most of the factories commenced work about the first of September. One or two began operations during the early part of August. There was a new factory at Odessa and also one at Independence."

KANSAS.

" The crop was late. Several factories did not pack so that there was a deficiency of 19,867 cases as compared with the small total of last year."

THE SOUTH.

" There have been a large number of small factories started at various points in the Southern States. As a rule, these houses turn out a small quantity, say 1,000 to 1,500 cases, for which they find a local market. One factory in Georgia commenced in July and stopped in October with an output of 5,000 cases. Another in North Georgia also packed 5,000 cases. One of them put up 25,000 cases of peaches. The factory at Griffin, Ga., was discontinued. In Alabama the Tomato crop was a failure and almost nothing was done in Texas and Arkansas."

OHIO.

" The crop was very good in quality, but deficient in quantity. The season commenced from the 5th to the 20th of August."

VIRGINIA.

" There were quite a number of factories discontinued during the year. The season opened all the way from the first to the latter part of August, and closed at various dates in October. There was only a partial crop."

From the above report, which is as accurate as is available, we may learn that the consumption of Tomatoes is ahead of the productions averaged for the last six years. Also that the production fell short last year and the stock on hands will be consumed long before the new ones come into market. This means, as we reason, that the Tomato growing and canning business is likely to be good for several years to come.

Another thing is clear from this report, viz : That " high grade goods " are in demand. Of course there is more *risk* to aim for this, but there is also more *gain* if you can make it win.

The prospect for Tomato culture, in my judgment, was never more flattering. There is no end to newer and better developments in the business in kinds, culture, appliances, harvesting and selling. I was much interested in a statement in a recent number of the Rural New Yorker, as illustrative of " something new," which I here give as follows :

" It occurred to the writer last year that the Tomato might possibly be induced to become a tuber-bearing plant. IIe reasoned that the Tomato berry or fruit is structurally the same as the potato berry or fruit ; that the wild potato bears very small and very few tubers, while it bears lots of fruit ; that cultivation alone has reversed this, causing a"maximum of tuber and a minimum of fruit. Accordingly several Tomato plants set out last May have been disbudded as soon as the buds have appeared. The plants have grown to twice the usual size of those which are allowed to bloom, and to bear all the fruit they will. The effect on the roots is not yet known. Probably such plants will have to be propagated by cutting through several or many seasons, never allowing them to bloom, before it can be decided whether the Tomato may or may not be forced into a tuber-bearing plant. The suggestion is offered to our station experimentors for what it may be worth."

Would it not be strange indeed, if in a few years we were to have tuber-bearing Tomatoes as common on our markets, and as much sought after as the Irish potato is now? And yet stranger things have happened than this ! I trust the Rural and other reliable papers will follow this up till it is known what can be done for us all in this line.

Well, we have now been together for a long time, a whole season through, over these Tomato affairs in the world. I trust you *have been* not a little interested in reading and *will be* not a little profited by trying to do the things I have suggested to you on these pages.

ALPHABETICAL INDEX.

ALPHABETICAL INDEX.

ALPHABETICAL INDEX.

ALPHABETICAL INDEX.

APPENDIX

NINETEENTH-CENTURY
TOMATO VARIETIES IN AMERICA

Tomatoes were marketed under a variety of names during the nineteenth century. Many names were synonyms. Seedsmen made more money by issuing new names to old tomatoes. Even those varieties that were genuinely different did not survive for long periods of time. Some varieties, for instance, were novelties and usually had a very short life. Below are listed tomato varieties cited in seed catalogues, agricultural and gardening publications, and books and pamphlets published before 1900. While this list is by no means comprehensive, it does offer a general overview of tomato varieties offered for sale before the twentieth century.

Acme (Livingston's). Introduced by Livingston in 1875. Medium-sized, uniformly smooth, slightly depressed at the ends, early tomato; very tender and fine flesh, solid, and delicate in flavor. Highly subject to rot; fruit sometimes very soft and watery when fully ripe. Its peculiar color, pinkish red, was objected to by many people. Plants were of strong and vigorous growth, very productive; fruit ripened all over and through at the same time. Had good carrying qualities, an important requisite for a desirable market variety, and was unequaled for canning, preserving, or slicing. It was well adapted for southern culture, and one of the best to grow for the northern market. According to Bailey, the **Acme** was "one of the best varieties in cultivation." Popular 1879–1930. Similar to **Beauty, Buist's Beauty, Burpee's Climax, Climax, Essex Hybrid, Hovey,** and **Rochester** or **Rochester Favorite.**

Sources: *Prairie Farmer* 48 (August 11, 1877): 250; *Gardener's Monthly* 25 (July 1883): 205, 368; Livingston's, 1887, 44; *Landreths' Seed Catalogue,* 1887, 57; Nicholson, 1887, 53; Bailey, 1887, 23; Buist, 1890, 102; Livingston, 1893, 25–27; Gould, 1974, 4.

Advance. Fruit red or yellowish red. A small sort like Hathaway's **Excelsior,** but earlier. The plant was lower and smaller, and the fruit usually 2 inches or less in diameter. Recommended for early use. Similar to **Extra Early Advance.**

Sources: Bailey, 1887, 22; *Garden and Forest* 2 (November 27, 1889): 576.

Alger. Originated with Oliver Alger of Cleveland about 1852. It was a chance sprout from the old **Large Red.** Occasionally irregular, the fruit was generally early, smooth, and round. Foliage was very dark green and of a more vigorous habit; productive. One observer wrote in 1870: "Of all the sorts yet named and introduced, my garden (whether I should want to grow for sale or family use) needs no other variety." Used for table or canning purposes.

Sources: Vick, 1869, 94–95; *Prairie Farmer* 40 (September 4, 1870): 275.

Alpha. Favored for form, color, solidity, evenness in ripening, and good flavor. Popular 1882–83. Similar to **Boston Market, Fulton Market, Extra Early Red,** and **General Grant.**

Sources: *American Agriculturist* 37 (November 1878): 407; Gould, 1974, 4.

Annie Dine. A new variety with some of the characteristics of the **Mikado,** having the pinkish color and very large size of that variety. It was one of the first varieties to become soft after picking, which meant that it was unsuccessful as a commercial plant.

Source: Sturtevant, 1889, 41.

Apfel Weisser. See **White Apple.**

Apple-Shaped. Medium-sized, somewhat flattened, inclining to globular, depressed about the stem, but smooth and regular in its outline; early, hardy, productive, kept well, and, for salad and certain forms of cookery, was "much esteemed; but it is more liable to be hallow-hearted than any other of the large varieties." Thick, tough rind.

Variously sized and shaped fruit. The monstrous or overgrown specimens developed "a scar-like line or ring on the top and ends of the fruit turning downwards." The **Improved Apple** differed little in appearance from the **Apple-Shaped.** Its superiority consisted in its much greater solidity, the absence of the tough rind, and the less seedy and more pulpy character of its flesh. The color of the **Improved Apple** was also deeper; it ripened earlier, was uniform in size and smoothness. Recommended for general cultivation. Similar to **Baltimore Prize Taker.**

Sources: Burr, 1863, 635–36, 643; Washburn & Company, 1869, 124.

Arlington. Introduced in 1873 by B. K. Bliss & Son, of New York. It was a good, solid tomato, but matured too late and had a freckled appearance. Fruit uniformly large, perfect in form; very prolific, and of fine flavor. Popular 1874–78. Similar to **Roseborough** and **Paragon.**

Sources: *Prairie Farmer* 44 (March 22, 1873): 89; *American Farmer*, 8th ser., 3 (December 1873): 422–23; Henderson, 1876, 15; Gould, 1974, 4.

Atlantic Prize. An early, smooth, red sort, very productive. The vine was short-lived and lacking in vigor. Too rough to be salable after the smoother sorts reached market. Popular 1891–1907.

Sources: *Landreths' American Grown Seeds,* 1897, 50; Bailey, 1910, p. 1814; Gould, 1974, 4.

Baltimore Prize Taker. A large, apple-shaped tomato. It was smooth, solid, coreless, and ripened all over; red color with slight purple tint; very productive and commanded quick sale in market.

Source: *Landreths' American Grown Seeds,* 1897, 50.

Barley Cluster. See **Extra Early.**

Beauty (Livingston's). Introduced by Livingston in 1886. A variation of the **Paragon** type. Beautiful color and appearance, whence it takes its name. Grew in clusters of four or five on a strong vine; fruit was showy and retained large size up to the end of the season—an essential point in its favor, as many other good sorts decreased in size by at least a half before the season was over. Uniform and smooth large fruit. Productive: yielded one-third more than the **Acme** and was free from rot. Withstood long shipments to market without injury. The color was a very glossy crimson with a slight tinge of purple. Thick skinned with few seeds. Solid and meaty, smooth, and free from rot or green core, seldom cracked after a rain. Unsurpassed for shipping and early market because of its solidity, its toughness of skin, and especially its purple color. It could be picked quite green and still ripen nicely. According to Livingston, the **Beauty** was sold in Chicago as the **Acme,** in Detroit as the **Fejee,** in Baltimore as the **Prize Taker.** Popular 1887–1929.

Sources: Nellis, 1886, 92; *Landreths' Seed Catalogue,* 1887, 16; Livingston's, 1887, 44; *Garden and Forest* 5 (October 12, 1892): 488; Livingston, 1893, 31, 35; *Landreths' American Grown Seeds,* 1897, 50; Gould, 1974, 4.

Beefsteak. See **Fejee.**

Belle. A hybrid of Livingston's **Beauty.** Fruit was solid, larger in size, well shaped, with a beautiful bright scarlet color. Tomatoes weighed 1½ pounds each.

Source: Buist, 1890, 102.

Bermuda Extra Early. A red- or rose-colored, apple-shaped variety, extensively imported from Bermuda into the middle and northern states in May and the early summer months. It varied considerably in size. It possessed a thick, rather tough rind, useful for long shipment. The fruit rarely became pulpy in the process of cooking. Light, hollow fruit. It was not successfully grown in the United States. Similar to **Apple-Shaped, Early Richmond,** and **Large Red.**

Sources: Burr, 1863, 643–44; *Landreths' Seed Catalogue,* 1887, 16; Bailey, 1887, 18.

Blounts' Champion Cluster. Fruit grew in clusters of ten to twenty large-sized, smooth, well-shaped fruits in one bunch. Similar to **Trophy.**

Source: Henderson, 1876, 15.

Boston Market. Unsurpassed as a large, smooth variety for market purposes. Red or yellowish red in color. Fruit flattened, in average specimens about 3 inches broad the longest way by 1½ inches deep; somewhat cornered, but firm. The fruit inclined to become double and distorted. Similar to **Alpha, Extra Early Red, Fulton Market,** and **General Grant.**

Sources: Gregory, 1872, 19; Bailey, 1887, 20.

Brandywine. Bright red, broad fruit, slightly flattened; productive and satisfactory.

Source: *Landreths' American Grown Seeds,* 1897, 50.

Bronze Foliage Trophy. Fruit red or yellowish red. Stems, veins on the underside of the young leaves, and leaf margins colored with dark violet; the leaves were a darker dull green compared with other plants. When the plants were young, the bronze was very marked. Throughout the season, the darker color was noticeable at some distance. Similar to **Trophy.**

Source: Bailey, 1887, 21.

Buckeye State (Livingston's). Introduced by Livingston in 1893. Very large, round, heavy, smooth, and solid tomato, purple in color. Fruit may have weighed 1½ pounds apiece. Ripened early and was good for home use. Popular 1895–1915.

Sources: Munson, 1893, 118; *Garden and Forest* 7 (February 14, 1894): 70; *Landreths' American Grown Seeds,* 1897, 50; Gould, 1974, 4.

Buist's Beauty. Introduced by Buist in 1888. Originated on Buist's Rosedale farm from a cross made between Livingston's **Paragon** and Livingston's **Perfection.** Fruit was solid, large in size, perfect in shape, and brilliant scarlet in color. Few seeds and no hard core. It

ripened evenly without cracking or wrinkling. Profitable market variety. Similar to Livingston's **Beauty.**
Source: Buist, 1890, 102.

Buist's Selected Trophy. See **Trophy.**

Burpee's Climax. See **Acme.**

Bush. See **French Upright.**

Canada Victor. Introduced by J. H. Gregory of Marblehead, Mass., who purchased a few seeds from a Canadian for $1,000. An early tomato, named by a market gardener who visited Gregory. Large size, about 4 inches broad by 2 inches deep, bright red color, symmetrical, uniform smoothness. In ripening, free from green or cracking around the stem; ripe seven days earlier than other tomato varieties then available. First-class cropping qualities. Lacked thick, green, heavy rind around the stem, thus bringing back a feature of the tomato found near old Mexican camping grounds in Texas and New Mexico. Much more acidic and not as good in flavor as the **Trophy.** Some held it to be a second-rate tomato: not by any means an early variety, too wrinkled, inconstant in size and shape, usually considerably flattened, with no superior merits. Popular 1874–92. Same as **Cook's Favorite.**
Sources: *American Agriculturist* 32 (March 1873): 104; *American Farmer,* 8th ser., 3 (December 1873): 422–23; *Prairie Farmer* 44 (February 1, 1873): 34, 40; *Prairie Farmer* 44 (April 19, 1873): 122; *Prairie Farmer* 45 (April 4, 1874): 105; Henderson, 1876, 15; *Gardener's Monthly* 25 (October 1883): 301; Bailey, 1887, 20; Gould, 1974, 4.

Cardinal. Fruit brilliant red in color; flesh solid, smooth, early, fair-sized, free from seeds, and of a pure, rich flavor. Popular 1887–88. Similar to **Queen.**
Sources: Livingston's, 1887, 44; Buist, 1890, 103; Gould, 1974, 4.

Carter's Green Gage. See **Green Gage, Ivory Ball,** or **White Apple.**

Cedar Hill. Originated before 1860 with John Sill of Cedar Hill, N. Y. An early sort and superior to other varieties in every respect. The fruit was of a medium to large, uniform size, distinct in appearance; it was tolerably smooth and had few seeds. Free from indentations; known for productiveness, solidity, and good flavor. An abundant bearer, it continued to produce fruit until cut down by October frosts. Sill grew the variety extensively for the Albany market and found it more profitable than any other. Similar to **Hundred Days.** Popular 1872–73.

Sources: *Horticulturist* 22 (December 1867): 366; Washburn & Company, 1869, 134–35; Vick, 1869, 94–95; *Prairie Farmer* 44 (March 22, 1873): 89; *Horticulturist* 28 (July 1873): 200; Bailey, 1887, 17; Gould, 1974, 4.

Cerise. See **Cherry (Yellow).**

Champion. See **Queen.**

Chemin. Recommended for hothouse growing in the Boston area.
Sources: *Garden and Forest* 7 (October 24, 1894): 428; *Garden and Forest* 8 (June 26, 1895): 257–58.

Cherry (Red). A small, round, red fruit the shape and size of a cherry. The earliest of all tomatoes. Quite small; flavor unsurpassed. Produced in great profusion, in large bunches or clusters, but was of comparatively little value on account of its small size. Used as a preserve and for pickling. With its size and sprightly acid flavor, it made an excellent pickle. More ornamental than useful. During the late nineteenth century these small sorts were more popular in Europe than in the U.S. Called the **Rothe Kirsch** in Germany and the **Cerise** in France; both averaged somewhat larger fruit. Popular in the U.S. from the 1840s to the present.
Sources: Dunlap & Thomson, 1847, 6; Buist, 1847, 126; Com-

stock, Ferre & Company, 1852, 43; Burr, 1863, 649; *Scientific American,* n. s., 17 (August 3, 1867): 73–74; W. White, 1868, 313; Gregory, 1872, 18; Henderson, 1876, 15; Bailey, 1887, 13; Gould, 1974, 4.

Cherry (Yellow). Like the **Red Cherry,** except lemon yellow in color. Uniformly oval and perfectly smooth in shape; used for making preserves, pickles, and tomato figs. The **Gelbe Kirsch** from Prussia averaged fruits twice as large as those in the U.S., but had a tendency to become irregular. Popular 1887–1930.

Sources: Comstock, Ferre & Company, 1852, 43; Thorburn, 1862, 21; Burr, 1863, 652; *Prairie Farmer* 19 (April 23, 1867): 223; Bailey, 1887, 13; Gould, 1974, 4.

Chiswick Red. See **King Humbert** and **President Garfield.**

Cincinnati Purple. Large pink-fruited variety of rich flavor. Very productive, but rarely ripened up to the stem; generally the upper third of the fruit turned a yellowish red color without becoming fully ripe. Especially adapted for canning and shipping. Highly recommended by growers. Popular 1887–96.

Sources: Sturtevant, 1889, 4; McCullough, 1890, 85; Gould, 1974, 4.

Climax (Burpee's). See **Acme.**

Cluster. See **Blounts' Champion Cluster, Crimson Cluster, Ford's Cluster, Lyman's Mammoth Cluster, Mammoth Cluster, New Cluster, Red Valencia Cluster,** and **Sim's Early Cluster.** For **Early Cluster,** see **Extra Early.**

College. Originated at the Michigan Agricultural College (today Michigan State University) in 1863. It was a seedling of the **Early Red.** Smooth and symmetrical fruit of medium size with unusual foliage.

Source: *Prairie Farmer* 20 (October 26, 1867): 262.

Collins. See **Eureka.**

Conqueror. Introduced in 1874. One of the very earliest and a quite productive variety. Large fruit (often 3 to 4 in. or more in circumference), variable and irregular in size, oblong in shape, bright dark red in color, and densely sprinkled, especially below, with very small golden yellow dots. Ripened evenly and regularly. Said to be a cross between the **General Grant** and **Keyes' Early Prolific.** Popular 1876–93.

Sources: Henderson, 1876, 15; Bailey, 1887, 17; Buist, 1890, 103; Gould, 1974, 4.

Cook's Favorite. Introduced by C. N. Brackett or H. A. Dreer in 1864. Originated in Burlington County, N.J. Handsome fruit of a deep red color and remarkable solidity; medium-sized, roundish or oval, smooth. Flesh firm and containing little water and few seeds compared with most varieties. Kept longer after being gathered and good for transport; rarely found with a cavity or hard, unripe parts at the center. Plants were strong and vigorous with fine, broad, light green foliage and bore abundantly. Very thick between the blossom and the stem ends. Popular in the middle states, where it yielded abundantly; extensively grown in the vicinity of New York, southern New Jersey, and Philadelphia by market gardeners and for supplying the large canning establishments. Free from the seams or creases so objectionable in some varieties. Ten years after its introduction, it was rechristened the **Canada Victor.** Differed little from the **Early Smooth Red,** except in shape of the fruit.

Sources: Dreer, 1864, 21; Burr, 1865, 639; Henderson, 1867, 217; *Landreths' Rural Register,* 1868, 56, 62–63; *Tilton's Journal of Horticulture* 4 (November 1868): 276; Henderson, 1876, 15; Bailey, 1887, 20; *Landreths' Seed Catalogue,* 1887, 57; *American Gardening* 16 (June 5, 1895): 214–15; Benson, 1929, 140.

Crimson Cluster. Originated in 1867 by Robert Revelle of Norwich, Conn. Novelty was that the fruit formed in clusters of fifteen to thirty tomatoes resembling a bunch of grapes but with berries of mammoth proportions. Each bunch or cluster averaged from 4 to 6 pounds. The fruit was smooth, of scarlet crimson color, delicately tinted with specks of golden yellow. It was a highly ornamental plant when trained against a trellis or wall.

Sources: *Horticulturist* 24 (January 1869): 12; Gregory, 1872, 18.

Criterion (Vick's). Pink-purple fruit averaged 2 to 2½ inches deep and 2 inches broad; more or less squared at the ends. Occasionally, the fruit broadened, becoming three times wider than deep.

Source: Bailey, 1887, 14.

Crystal. An English variety. Good-sized, solid, and highly recommended.

Source: *Ohio Farmer* 13 (April 30, 1864): 139.

Cuba. See **Cherry.**

Currant. *Lycopersicon pimpinellifolium.* The smallest sort grown. The red fruit hung in long clusters and looked very much like long bunches of currants. Very ornamental and quite a contribution to decorations for the table. Useful for preserving. See also **Grape.**

Sources: Gregory, 1872, 10, 19; Henderson, 1876, 15; Livingston's, 1887, 45.

Dixie. Fruit weighed 16 ounces and measured 14 inches. It was uniformly large, though not uniformly smooth and round. Prolific with productive yield.

Source: *Tilton's Journal of Horticulture* 5 (April 1869): 243.

Dreer's Extra Early. See **Extra Early.**

Dreer's Selected Trophy. See **Trophy.**

Dwarf Aristocrat (Livingston's). Introduced by Livingston in 1893. Bright glossy red color, very fine flesh and flavor, uniformly smooth. Small but uniform fruit, round and solid. Valuable variety for amateurs. Popular 1893–1903.

Sources: Livingston, 1893, 42; *Garden and Forest* 7 (February 14, 1894): 70; Gould, 1974, 4.

Dwarf Champion. Introduced 1888. Smooth fruit, nearly round, solid, of medium to large size. Crimson in color tinged with purple, and of good flavor. Foliage dark, almost of a bluish cast, very curled and twisted leaves, of upright growth and great vigor. The bush was compact and the plant easily staked. It was difficult to prune, however, because the heavy leaves hid the sprouts. Stems short, thick, stiff, almost self-supporting. Easy to transplant. Bore heavily all through the season. Fit for shipping on account of its tough skin. Popular 1889–1936. See also **Acme.**

Sources: *American Agriculturist* 48 (February 1889): 81; *Garden and Forest* 2 (May 22, 1889): 245; *Garden and Forest* 3 (June 4, 1890): 276; *Garden and Forest* 4 (February 11, 1891): 68; *Garden and Forest* 5 (October 12, 1892): 488; Wickson, 1897, 294; *Landreths' American Grown Seeds,* 1897, 50; Bailey, 1901, 402; Gould, 1974, 4.

Dwarf Orangefield. Medium size. Most useful and suited for cultivation in the United Kingdom. Popular 1872–74. See also **Orangefield.**

Sources: *Horticulturist* 28 (July 1873): 200; Anderson, 1874, 206; Gould, 1974, 4.

Dwarf Red. Used for culinary purposes; dwarf, bushy growth.

Source: Dreer, 1864, 21.

Earley's Defiance. A hybrid of the **Orangefield** and the **Large Red Italian** with the yields of the former and the brilliant red color of the latter.

Source: Anderson, 1874, 206.

Early Advance. See **Advance.**

Early Bermuda. See **Bermuda Extra Early.**

Early Canada Victor. See **Canada Victor.**

Early Cluster. See **Extra Early.**

Early Conqueror. See **Conqueror.**

Early Dwarf Red. Fruit normally about 2 inches across by 1 inch deep; dark orange red, conspicuously angled or even cornered. Also called **Rouge Naine Hâtive** and **Frühe Rothe Zwerg.**
Source: Bailey, 1887, 18.

Early Jersey. Earliest of all, good size, solid and fairly smooth, color red. Vines very closely jointed and compact; suitable for close planting. Fruit borne near the root and in clusters of sometimes fifty or sixty tomatoes to a vine. Desirable as a first early.
Sources: *Landreths' Seed Catalogue,* 1887, 16; *Landreths' American Grown Seeds,* 1897, 50.

Early Michigan. Popular 1889–1930. Also known as **Early Red Apple** before 1891.
Source: Gould, 1974, 4.

Early Paragon. See **Paragon.**

Early Red. A French subvariety of **Large Red.** See also **College.**
Sources: Thorburn, 1862, 2; W. White, 1868, 313.

Early Red Apple. Popular 1889–91; renamed **Early Michigan** in 1891.
Source: Gould, 1974, 4.

Early Richmond. Early, bright red, and productive, but crooked and hollow. Scarcely distinguishable from the **Large Red.** Similar to **Bermuda Extra Early** and **Extra Early Richmond.**
Sources: *American Farmer,* 8th ser., 3 (December 1873): 422–23; Bailey, 1887, 17.

Early Smooth Red. Medium-sized, rich coral red, roundish, much flattened, apple-shaped, solid. Very smooth but rather small. Yielded the greatest amount of marketable fruit. Seedsman Peter Henderson of New York recommended it as the most productive marketable tomato of the early varieties. A very old variety used for general crop and market purposes.

Sources: *American Agriculturist* 25 (January 1866): 21; Henderson, 1867, 216–17; Vick, 1869, 94–95; *Prairie Farmer* 43 (November 23, 1872): 372; *Horticulturist* 28 (July 1873): 200; *Florida Agriculturist* 1 (May 9, 1874): 150–51; Henderson, 1876, 15; Buist, 1890, 103.

Early Trophy. Popular in 1881.
Source: Gould, 1974, 4.

Early York. Very early, dwarf, and productive. Similar to **Extra Early York.**
Source: Gregory, 1872, 18.

Eclipse. A splendid English sort recommended for growing under glass in Boston area.
Source: *Garden and Forest* 8 (June 26, 1895): 257–58.

Egg-Shaped. See **Pear-Shaped.**

Einformige Dauer. Uniform in size and shape, with average specimens measuring nearly 2 inches across. Conspicuously angled, often nearly square; firm; very bright orange-red.
Source: Bailey, 1887, 17.

Emery. Fine for early market. See also **Paragon.**
Source: Schlegel, 1878, 16.

English Large Red. See **Large Red.**

English's Seedling. Medium and small sizes turned out well; the large monstrosities were deeply ribbed and knotted.
Source: *Gardener's Monthly & Horticultural Advertiser* 10 (January 1868): 10–11.

Essex Early Round. Very early, round, and solid. Differed from the **Red Valencia Cluster** in its smaller size. Similar to **Essex Round Red Smooth.**
Sources: Gregory, 1872, 18; Bailey, 1887, 21.

Essex Hybrid. Introduced in 1867 by Jonathan Periam of the Tremont Gardens, Chicago. The fruit, which grew in clusters, was medium-sized, smooth, roundish, generally solid, and of a pale red color. The plant was a dwarf, bush-shaped, upright, an early and robust grower; resembled the **French Tree** tomato, to which it was closely related. Too small to be profitably grown as a market sort, but the dwarf, stocky habit of the plant, together with its beauty when loaded with numerous clusters of ripe fruit, made it a favorite with those who wished to combine the ornamental with the useful. Similar to the **Foard** and **Maupay's Superior.**
Sources: *Prairie Farmer* 19 (April 23, 1867): 223; *Tilton's Journal of Horticulture* 4 (December 1868): 329; Vick, 1869, 94–95; Washburn & Company, 1869, 134–35.

Essex Round Red Smooth. See **Essex Early Round.**

Eureka. Originated with Major Kendall of Philadelphia and introduced by Jonathan Periam of Chicago, who considered it "superior to any thing I have ever tried; dwarf, early, bush-shape, and prolific, Tree, or Erect." By selection and proper training, it reached an upright, robust habit, and was productive. The plant was extremely compact, rigid, and dwarf; ornamental with very dark foliage and curious growth. Similar to **Collins, Foard,** and **Maupay's Superior.**
Sources: *Prairie Farmer* 19 (April 23, 1867): 223; *Prairie Farmer* 20 (October 26, 1867): 262; *Rural New Yorker* 19 (September 12, 1868): 295; *Tilton's Journal of Horticulture* 4 (December 1868): 329; Washburn & Company, 1869, 134–35.

Excelsior (Hathaway's). Originated in America and found its way to England. Early, productive, bright red or yellowish red, medium-sized (1½–2½ inches in diameter), round, smooth, very solid, and of excellent quality. Fruit grew in clusters and cracked badly when ripe. Suitable for market and also for canning. Appears to be a direct development of **Cherry** or **Plum**. Popular 1873–86. Similar to **New Red Apple** and Livingston's **Favorite**.

Sources: *Prairie Farmer* 44 (March 22, 1873): 89; *Horticulturist* 28 (July 1873): 200; *Horticulturist* 28 (December 1873): 376; Henderson, 1876, 15; Schlegel, 1878, 16; *Gardener's Monthly* 25 (July 1883): 205, 368; *Gardener's Monthly* 25 (October 1883): 301; Bailey, 1887, 21–22; *Landreths' Seed Catalogue,* 1887, 57; Buist, 1890, 103; Hedrick, 1919, 346; Gould, 1974, 4.

Extra Early. Originated in France; introduced into America by Landreth about 1853. Red colored. Used for culinary purposes. Long cultivated as the earliest variety; desirable only before others mature. See also **One Hundred Days** and **Round (Red)**.

Sources: *Landreths' Seed Catalogue,* 1859, 18; Dreer, 1864, 21; *Landreths' Rural Register,* 1868, 62–63; *Landreths' Seed Catalogue,* 1887, 56.

Extra Early Advance (Burpee's). Early, small, solid fruit, bright red color, uniform size. Shape not far removed from the **Cherry** tomato. See also **Advance.**

Sources: Burpee, 1888, 66; *Garden and Forest* 7 (February 14, 1894): 70.

Extra Early Red (Ferry's). Popular in the U.S. from 1868 to 1888. Similar to **Boston Market.**

Source: Gould, 1974, 4.

Extra Early Richmond. Early, fair size, solid but not smooth fruit. Good shipper. See also **Early Richmond** and **Bermuda Extra Early.**

Sources: *Landreths' Seed Catalogue,* 1887, 57; *Landreths' American Grown Seeds,* 1897, 50.

Extra Early York. See **Early York.**

Extra Mammoth. See **Mammoth Red.**

Farquhar's Faultless. See **Faultless.**

Faultless. Fruit red or yellowish red; rough. Similar to **Boston Market** and **Farquhar's Faultless.**
Sources: Bailey, 1887, 20; Burpee, 1888, 66.

Favorite (Livingston's). Introduced by Livingston in 1883. Large, meaty, perfectly shaped fruit; dark red color; ripened even and early. Good flavor, with solid, thick flesh and few seeds. Most prolific, with no open spaces between the seeds, ridges, or hollows from the stem to the blossom ends. Withstood shipping long distance and had desirable market characteristics. Developed especially for canners. Popular 1883–1907. See also **Cook's Favorite.**
Sources: *Landreths' Seed Catalogue,* 1887, 57; Livingston's, 1887, 44; *Garden and Forest* 2 (November 27, 1889): 576; Livingston, 1893, 30; *Landreths' American Grown Seeds,* 1897, 50; Gould, 1974, 4.

Fejee, Feejee, Fiji, or **Fejee Island.** Name first applied to tomatoes sent from Fiji by Commander Charles Wilkes in 1841, but these seeds had no discernible effect on tomato culture in the U.S. First offered in seed catalogues in 1862. An alternate explanation of origin: A Captain Frazier of Baltimore claimed to have discovered it in the Fiji Islands. He may have obtained it in Valparaiso or some other South American port, but even that is questionable, since the South Americans have no native sorts approximating the old **Fejee.** A third explanation is that it was introduced from Naples into Athens, Ga., about 1848. It grew in clusters and was an abundant bearer; large size (weighing 24½ oz.), thick, firm and very heavy flesh, few seeds, often blushed or tinged with pinkish crimson, flattened, sometimes ribbed and rough, often smooth, well filled to the center, and well flavored. The plant was hardy, healthy, and a strong grower, somewhat late in ripening, commonly irregular, often more or less contorted, and bearing elongated leaves of a silvery green. Desirable for culinary purposes; the best for family use, for putting up in cans for winter use, particularly good for pickling. Probably the first pink tomato. The purple-skinned sort was the forebearer of all other purple sorts, such as the **Essex, Acme, Beauty,** and others. Popular in the U.S. 1868–83. Similar to **Beefsteak** and **Lester's Perfected.**

Sources: *The World,* August 21, 1860, p. 6; *Rural New Yorker* 11 (September 8, 1860): 287; *Cultivator* 8 (November 1860): 357; Thorburn, 1862, 21; Burr, 1863, 644; Dreer, 1864, 2; Henderson, 1867, 218; *Gardener's Monthly & Horticultural Advertiser* 10 (January 1868): 10–11; W. White, 1868, 313; *Tilton's Journal of Horticulture* 3 (April 1868): 243–44; *Horticulturist* 28 (July 1873): 200; U.S. Department of Agriculture, 1875, 365–68; Nellis, 1884, 85; Bailey, 1887, 23; *Landreths' Seed Catalogue,* 1887, 57; *American Gardening* 16 (June 5, 1895): 214–15; Klose, 1950, 29; Gould, 1974, 4.

Ferry's Improved Early Large Smooth Red. See **Extra Early Red.**

Fig-Shaped. Red or yellow, pear-shaped, measuring from 1¼ to 1½ inches in length, and nearly 1 inch in diameter at its broadest. When dried, used as a sweetmeat. Flesh pale red or pink, very solid and compact, generally completely filling the center of the fruit. Uniform in size and shape, but little used except for preserving. Also known as **Wonder of Italy** and **Rothe Birne.**

Sources: Burr, 1863, 644–45; *Scientific American,* n. s., 17 (August 3, 1867): 73–74; Gregory, 1872, 18; Bailey, 1887, 13–14.

Fiji. See **Fejee.**

Fire King. Oval shape, small to medium size, deep red color.

Source: Sturtevant, 1889, 41.

Foard. Originated with a market gardener, Mr. Foard, in the vicinity of Philadelphia; introduced by Robert Buist of Philadelphia. Large fruit, deep red or bright scarlet color, early, flesh solid and well flavored. It cut as solidly as a well-ripened apple and was almost entirely

194
APPENDIX

free of seeds, which were concentrated mostly on one side of the fruit.
Similar to the **Eureka** and **Maupay's Superior.**

Sources: *Prairie Farmer* 20 (October 26, 1867): 262; *Tilton's Journal of Horticulture* 2 (December 1867): 357; *Practical Farmer* 5 (December 1868): 183; Washburn & Company, 1869, 134–35.

Ford's Cluster. Found growing in a **Trophy** tomato patch by John Ford of Detroit in 1871. Introduced in 1874. Early, very smooth, fair-sized, and free of hard, woody pulp.

Sources: *Gardener's Monthly* 16 (October 1874): 314-15; *Horticulturist* 30 (January 1875): 23.

Franz Grosse Rothe. See **Large Red.**

Sources: *Gardener's Monthly* 16 (October 1874): 314–15; *Horticulturist* 30 (January 1875): 23.

French Jaune Ronde Grosse. See **Large Yellow.**

French Upright, Upright, or **French Tree.** Raised from seed by Grenier, gardener to M. de Fleurieux, at Chateau de Laye near Villefranche, France, about 1837; introduced by M. Vilmorin of Paris. Introduced into the United States about 1858. The fruit was bright red or yellowish red, large-sized, solid and well filled to the center; it was very irregular on the sides and base, cornered, and flattened. The plant was quite erect to a height of 2 feet or more, with a stem of remarkable size and strength. The branches were not numerous and comparatively short, usually 8 or 10 inches in length. The leaves were not abundant, but rather curled, much wrinkled, very firm, closely placed on the sturdy branches, and of a remarkably deep shining green color. It was a slow grower: tardy in forming and perfecting its fruit. The **French Upright** was well adapted for cultivation in pots, but its late maturity greatly impaired its value as a variety for forcing. Grown mainly in private gardens as a useful curiosity. Also called **Tomate de Laye, Tree Tomato,** and **Tomate à Tige Roide.**

Sources: *American Agriculturist* 20 (February 1861): 50–51; *American Agriculturist* 21 (May 1862): 123; *American Agriculturist*

21 (August 1862): 230; Burr, 1863, 650; Henderson, 1867, 218; Gregory, 1872, 10; Bailey, 1887, 25; *Garden and Forest* 2 (September 4, 1889): 432.

Frühe Rothe Zwerg. See **Early Dwarf Red.**

Fulton Market. See **Boston Market.**

Funchal. Originated by John Sill of Cedar Hill, N. Y., who reported that its parent was **General Grant.**
Source: *Prairie Farmer* 44 (March 22, 1873): 89.

Gallagher's Mammoth. Large red fruit with few seeds and good flavor.
Source: W. White, 1868, 313.

Gelbe Kirsch. See **Cherry (Yellow).**

General Grant. Originated with an amateur; introduced in 1869. The fruit was above medium size, measuring from 3 to 4 inches in diameter, round, slightly flattened, very regular, symmetrical, rarely ribbed or wrinkled but smooth and shiny; grew in clusters. Dark, brilliant crimson in color; unusually firm, solid flesh, free of water, with few seeds and well flavored. It was medium early and productive, and remained in good condition a long time after gathering. Favored by market men and canners and valuable for shipping. Popular 1871–83.
Sources: *Tilton's Journal of Horticulture* 3 (February 1868): 88–89; *Horticulturist* 25 (February 1870): 51; Gregory, 1872, 18; U.S. Department of Agriculture, 1875, 365–68; Henderson, 1876, 15; Manning, 1880, 370; *Landreths' Seed Catalogue,* 1887, 57; Benson, 1929, 157; Gould, 1974, 4.

Gestreifte (Striped). Fruit streaked and splashed with irregular lines of orange or red stripes. See also **Golden Striped.**
Source: Bailey, 1887, 18.

Giant. Improved version of the **Large Red.** Not early, fruit solid, bright red, sometimes smooth, but generally ribbed and often exceedingly irregular. Fruit produced in clusters; flesh pale pink and well flavored. Under favorable conditions, 25 pounds to a single plant was not an unusual yield; single specimens of the fruit sometimes weighed 4 and even 5 or 6 pounds. Used for market, making ketchup, and pickles.

Source: Burr, 1863, 645.

Gold Ball (Livingston's). Introduced by Livingston in 1892. Bright golden yellow in color; round as a ball, 1½ inches in diameter; few seeds, fleshy, and extremely productive, yielding a half bushel per plant.

Source: Livingston, 1893, 39.

Golden Queen (Livingston's). Introduced by Livingston in 1884. Fruit yellow or yellowish white with a slight tendency to be reddish at the bottom; uniformly smooth, good size, flattish, reaching 2½ inches in diameter and often slightly angular. Most prolific and early ripening. Not very acidic; used for slicing or preserving, but valueless for cooking because it turned a brown muddy tint. Popular 1886–1936 and continues to be sold today.

Sources: Bailey, 1887, 19; Livingston's, 1887, 45; Sturtevant, 1889, 41; *Garden and Forest* 4 (February 11, 1891): 68; *Garden and Forest* 6 (April 26, 1893): 187; Livingston, 1893, 29–30; Bailey, 1910, p. 1815; Gibault, 1912, 376; Gould, 1974, 4.

Golden Striped. An eye-catching tomato with yellow and red stripes; fairly large size, of good quality and moderately productive. See also **Gestreifte.**

Sources: Vick, 1869, 94–95; *Horticulturist* 28 (July 1873): 200.

Golden Sunrise. See **Golden Queen.**

Golden Trophy. Fruit yellow or yellowish white often shading into orange or red; fruit large and solid, somewhat angular and irregular. A bright yellow type of **Trophy.** High yielding, ripening well up to the stem, a good keeper, and, all things considered, the best yellow tomato introduced before 1900. Used for preserving as well as for the table. Also called **Yellow Victor** and **Jaune Grosse Lisse.**

Sources: Bailey, 1887, 20; *Landreths' Seed Catalogue,* 1887, 57; Sturtevant, 1889, 41; Buist, 1890, 103; *Landreths' American Grown Seeds,* 1897, 50.

Grape, Currant, or **Cluster.** *Lycopersicon pimpinellifolium.* Different *Lycopersicon* species than other tomatoes listed here. The fruit was nearly globular, quite small, about ½ inch in diameter, of a bright, scarlet color, and produced in leafless, simple, or compound clusters. These were 6 or 8 inches in length and sported twenty to sixty tomatoes. The plants usually grew about 3 feet in length; were comparatively small, early, ornamental; and emitted little musky odor. The flowers were yellow; the leaves smoother and thinner in texture. Used for pickles and preserves.

Sources: Burr, 1863, 646; *Prairie Farmer* 20 (October 26, 1867): 262; *Landreths' Seed Catalogue,* 1887, 57; *Landreths' American Grown Seeds,* 1897, 50.

Great Chihuahua. See **Mammoth Chihuahua.**

Great Mammoth. See **Mammoth Red.**

Green Gage. Apple-shaped, cherry-like fruit (measuring about 1¼ or 1½ inches in diameter); some red in color, others yellow or yellowish white; mostly spherical, sometimes slightly oblong. Used for home use such as making pickles. Popular 1879–83. See also **Ivory Ball** and **White Apple.**

Sources: Nicholson, 1887, 53; Bailey, 1887, 19; Bailey, 1901, 402; Gould, 1974, 4.

Grosse Rouge Hâtive. See **Hubbard's Curled Leaf.**

Hathaway's Excelsior. See **Excelsior.**

Henderson's Extra Selected Trophy. See **Trophy.**

Honor Bright (Livingston's). Introduced in 1897. Early, medium-sized, nearly round, uniform, very productive, bearing fruit in large clusters. Fruit turned a lighter green in ripening, then became so light that one could call it white; subsequently turned yellow with darker spots about the stems. A faint blush then appeared, which deepened and spread until the whole fruit, when fully ripe, was light red. This ripening process took place very slowly, much more so than in any other variety. The flesh was very solid even when fully ripe, quite dry with little pulp, but abundant in seeds. Skin very hard and firm. Mild flavor. The fruit could be picked when yellow, packed in barrels, and sent long distances to ripen en route. The vine was strong growing and vigorous with large leaves of yellowish green color. Popular 1897–1909.

Sources: *Garden and Forest* 10 (November 17, 1897): 455; Gould, 1974, 4.

Horsford's Prelude. Introduced by Horsford & Pringle of Vermont. Productive, with as many as a dozen or more fruit in a cluster, hanging at regular intervals along the stem. The fruit was medium-sized, smooth, bright red, and succulent.

Source: *Garden and Forest* 1 (September 19, 1888): 352.

Hovey. See **Acme.**

Hubbard's Curled Leaf. Early, medium size, slightly ribbed, dwarf. Fruit larger than other dwarfs, but not so conspicuously squared; fruit variable in size and shape and approaching more nearly the character of the apple-shaped sorts. Popular 1872–86. Also called **Krausblätter** and **Grosse Rouge Hâtive.** Closely resembles **Early York.**

Sources: Gregory, 1872, 18; *Horticulturist* 28 (July 1873): 200; *Florida Agriculturist* 1 (May 9, 1874): 150–51; Henderson, 1876, 15; Bailey, 1887, 18; Gould, 1974, 4.

Hundert Tagige. See **Hundred Days.**

Hundred Days. Introduced by J. A. Foote in Terre Haute, Ind. Fruit 2–3 inches wide and usually less than 1½ inches deep, generally much angled, dark red. Popular 1876–90. Same as or similar to **Stamfordian** from Dickson, England, **One Hundred Days,** and **Hundert Tagige.**

Sources: *California Farmer* 44 (February 10, 1876): 163; *American Agriculturist* 36 (February 1877): 47; Bailey, 1887, 17; *Garden and Forest* 5 (October 12, 1892): 487–88; Gould, 1974, 4.

Ignotum. Found by L. H. Bailey about 1885 on the grounds of Michigan Agricultural College, which were planted with a small German variety, **Einformige Dauer.** Fruit red or yellowish red. Large to very large sized fruit: smooth, regular, solid, heavy, long-keeping. Stem 4 feet high, each produced 6 to 10 pounds of fruit. Never cracked, skin not thick. Good for forcing. Grown under glass at Cornell University. Popular 1889–98.

Sources: Bailey, 1887, 22; *Garden and Forest* 2 (September 4, 1889): 432; *Garden and Forest* 4 (February 11, 1891): 68; *Garden and Forest* 4 (February 17, 1892): 81; *Garden and Forest* 8 (February 13, 1895): 66; *Garden and Forest* 8 (June 19, 1895): 240; *Landreths' American Grown Seeds,* 1897, 50; Gould, 1974, 4.

Imperial. Popular 1896–98.
Source: Gould, 1974, 4.

Improved Apple. See **Apple.**

Improved Fejee Island. See **Fejee.**

Improved Large Yellow. See **Large Yellow.**

Improved Mansfield Tree. See **Mansfield Tree.**

Improved Mayflower. See **Mayflower.**

Island Beauty. See **Trophy.**

Ivory Ball. Small, round fruit (1½ in. in diameter); bone white color; early and productive. Used for preserving. See also **Green Gage** and **White Apple.**

Sources: *Landreths' Seed Catalogue,* 1887, 57; Sturtevant, 1889, 41; *Landreths' American Grown Seeds,* 1897, 50.

Jackson or **Jackson's Favorite.** Large, red-colored fruit, but the surface was usually covered with minute golden dots.
Source: Bailey, 1887, 17–18.

Jaune Grosse Lisse. See **Golden Trophy.**

Jaune Ronde Grosse. See **Large Yellow.**

Keyes' Early Prolific. Originated with Charles A. Keyes of Worcester, Mass.; introduced by Hovey & Company of Boston in 1866. Early, uniform, medium-sized fruit; solid, smooth, brilliant or light red color, and mild favored. Fruit roundish or slightly corrugated, produced in clusters that ripened uniformly on a vine, with the fruit not more than 18 inches from the root of the plant. The foliage was large and particular; leaves often measured 8 inches in length by 6 in breadth. Leaflets much curled, larger than in most of the group. Plant dwarf, compact and vigorous, productive. Foliage had no odor. Useful for forcing. Its lack of smoothness, beauty, and flavor made it unworthy of cultivation. Its principal drawback, perhaps, was its small size. Used for canning. Recommended for early market. Popular 1866–74.

Sources: *Tilton's Journal of Horticulture* 1 (June 1866): 364; *Prairie Farmer* 20 (October 26, 1867): 262; *Prairie Farmer* 20 (November 9, 1867): 294; *Ohio Farmer* 17 (February 29, 1868): 133; *Tilton's Journal of Horticulture* 3 (April 1868): 243–44; *Tilton's Journal of Horticulture* 4 (October 1868): 249; *Landreths' Rural Register,* 1868, 62–63; *Practical Farmer* 5 (December 1868): 183; Vick, 1869, 94–95; Gregory, 1872, 18; *Semi-Tropical California and Southern California Horticulturist* 4 (November 1881): 187; Bailey, 1887, 18; Wickson, 1897, 294; Gould, 1974, 4.

King Humbert. According to the *Rural New Yorker,* introduced

from England into the U.S. about 1884 by Trentham Fillbasket. Fruit 2½–3 inches deep by 1 or 1½ inches broad, fig-shaped, regular or nearly so; bright red, did not ripen simultaneously on the stem end. Flesh two- or three-celled and scarcely acid. Used for pickles and preserves. Often rotted before ripening. Similar to **Chiswick Red, Fig-Shaped,** and **President Garfield.**
Sources: Bailey, 1887, 14; Sturtevant, 1889, 41.

King of Earlies. Originated with Theodore F. Baker of Cumberland, N.J. Early, red, medium-sized.
Sources: *American Agriculturist* 48 (February 1889): 81; *Garden and Forest* 5 (October 12, 1892): 487–88.

Kirsch Rothe. See **Cherry (Red).**

Krausblätter. See **Hubbard's Curled Leaf.**

Ladybird. English variety introduced into the U.S. about 1895. Fine flavor but irregular fruit.
Source: *Garden and Forest* 8 (August 21, 1895): 336.

Large Red. Extensively used for market before 1870. Fruit from 3 to 18 inches in circumference. The earliest grew to a large size; color bright red when ripe; uneven shape and deeply furrowed, prolific; sometimes smooth, often irregular, flattened, more or less ribbed; very conspicuously angled and cornered, tending to bend downward at the ends and become ringed on top. Flesh pale red or rose color, solid; good flavor, produced from 12 to 15 pounds per plant. Largely grown as a late crop for making ketchup or preserving. See also **Large Red Oval Fruited.**
Sources: Buist, 1847, 126; Comstock, Ferre & Company, 1853, 43; *Landreths' Seed Catalogue,* 1859, 18; Burr, 1863, 646; Henderson, 1867, 218; *Scientific American,* n. s., 17 (August 3, 1867): 73–74; W. White, 1868, 312; *Landreths' Rural Register,* 1868, 56; *Gardener's Monthly & Horticultural Advertiser* 10 (January 1868): 10–11; *Til-*

ton's Journal of Horticulture 3 (April 1868): 243–44; Bailey, 1887, 17; *Landreths' Seed Catalogue,* 1887, 57.

Large Red Fejee. See **Fejee.**

Large Red Italian (Barr & Sugden's). Early, prolific, bearing fine fruit within 6 inches of the ground. Fruit very large, broad, red, and deeply corrugated or ribbed. Dwarf plant.
> Source: *Tilton's Journal of Horticulture* 3 (April 1868): 243–44.

Large Red Oval Fruited. Subvariety of **Large Red.** Liable to degenerate, constantly tending toward the **Large Red;** could only be maintained in its purity by exclusive cultivation and a continued use of seeds selected from the fairest, smoothest, best-ripened tomatoes with the peculiar oval shape.
> Source: Burr, 1863, 647.

Large Rose Peach (Livingston's). Introduced by Livingston in 1893. Grown in test fields for several years before it was introduced. Fruit large, mild tasting, and resistant to rot.
> Source: Livingston, 1893, 44–45.

Large Smooth Red. Appeared about 1853. Similar to the **Large Red,** but smooth and free from protuberances and indentations. Fruit smooth and fair, nearly round or flattened; bright red color. Pear-shaped was preferred for pickling, being more fleshy, firm, and pink. Used also for main crop.
> Sources: Buist, 1847, 126; Comstock, Ferre & Company, 1853, 43; Thorburn, 1862, 21; Dreer, 1864, 21; *Prairie Farmer* 19 (April 23, 1867): 223; W. White, 1868, 313; Gregory, 1872, 19.

Large Smooth Yellow. See **Large Yellow.**

Large White China Sugar. Popular in the U.S. in 1868.
> Source: Gould, 1974, 4.

Large Yellow, Pomo d'Oro, or **Golden Apple.** Bright semitransparent yellow color; about the size and shape of the **Large Red,** but a little more flat. Flesh yellow, firm, deeply corrugated, well filling the center, and sweeter or milder than the **Large Red.** The plant was very prolific, hardy, and yielded abundantly. Used for preserves. The **Improved Large Yellow** was yellow, yellowish white, or bright orange in color, darker than the **Large Yellow,** firmer and slightly angled. Valued only for home use, especially for making pickles. Designation as large was anomalous, as it was among the smallest varieties, but it was very regular in form, nearly globular, and kept sound a long time after picking. Called **Jaune Ronde Grosse** in French. Differed little from **Golden Trophy,** except averaged smaller in size of fruits.

Sources: Comstock, Ferre & Company, 1853, 43; Burr, 1863, 647; Henderson, 1867, 218; *Scientific American,* n. s., 17 (August 3, 1867): 73–74; W. White, 1868, 313; *Tilton's Journal of Horticulture* 3 (April 1868): 243–44; Gregory, 1872, 19; Henderson, 1876, 15; Bailey, 1887, 19; Sturtevant, 1889, 41.

Large York. Yellow, fair size, smooth, and of very good quality.
Source: *Horticulturist* 28 (July 1873): 200.

Lemon Blush (Thorburn's). Fruit medium size, bright lemon color with a faint blush, early and good.
Source: *Garden and Forest* 7 (February 14, 1894): 70.

Lester's Perfected. Light red or pinkish color, smooth, large, solid, few seeds; late. Used as main crop. See also **Fejee** and **Perfected.**
Sources: Thorburn, 1862, 21; Vick, 1869, 94–95; Gregory, 1872, 19; *Horticulturist* 28 (July 1873): 200.

Leverett. Originated with W. H. Lyman of Leverett, Mass.
Source: *Rural New Yorker* 19 (September 12, 1868): 295.

Little Gem. Fruit red or yellowish red. Small (1½–2 in. in diameter), regular, spherical or slightly flattened. A short remove from the cherry tomatoes. It differed from the **Large Yellow** only in color. Popular 1879–83.

Sources: Bailey, 1887, 20; Gould, 1974, 4.

Lorillard. Originated with John C. Gardener, former gardener of Pierre Lorillard of Jobstown, N.J., who crossed the **Acme** with the **Perfection;** introduced by A. D. Cowan & Company, New York, about 1889. Medium size, depressed globular, very firm and heavy, smooth; vermillion, scarlet, changing to a bluish tint when fully mature. It set freely with four or five fruit to a bunch, all remarkably uniform in shape and size. Ripened evenly; ripe fruits remained firm and solid when shipped. Used mainly for forcing.

Sources: *Garden and Forest* 2 (January 2, 1889): 5; *American Agriculturist* 48 (February 1889): 81; *American Agriculturist* 48 (March 1889): 123; *Garden and Forest* 4 (February 11, 1891): 68.

Lyman's Mammoth Cluster. Originated with W. H. Lyman, of Leverett, Mass., in 1868. Introduced by Vick in 1869. Fruit grew in large clusters, pinkish red in color.

Source: Vick, 1869, 95.

Mammoth Chihuahua. Fruit of mammoth proportions, but coarse, exceedingly irregular, and worthless. Same as **Great Chihuahua.**

Source: *Prairie Farmer* 20 (October 26, 1867): 262.

Mammoth Cluster. Large, round tomato that grew in clusters; a little hollow if not fully ripe.

Source: Gregory, 1872, 18.

Mammoth Red (Barr & Sugden's). Small and more finely cut leaves, with fruits very similar to those of **Grosse Rouge Hâtive.** Similar to **Great Mammoth** and **Large Red.**

Source: *Tilton's Journal of Horticulture* 3 (April 1868): 243–44.

Mansfield Tree. Said to grow to a height of 10 or 12 feet, and to produce fruit of an immense size and of the finest flavor. Ornamental as well as useful for the home. Fruit often measured over 6 inches in diameter and weighed over 3 pounds. Criticized as a humbug by some who never observed growth higher than 3 feet.

Sources: *Country Gentleman* 57 (February 4, 1892): 98; *American Gardening* 13 (April 1892): 224; *Country Gentleman* 58 (March 2, 1893): 169.

Market Champion. See **Queen.**

Matchless. Known for beauty of coloring and symmetry of form. Fruit large, entirely free of core, of a very rich cardinal red color, and not liable to crack from wet weather. Skin was remarkably tough and solid, so that ripe specimens picked from the vine kept in good marketable condition for more than two weeks. The vines were of strong, vigorous growth and well set with fruit; the foliage, very rich. Its fine quality, solidity, and long-keeping character were useful for both market and family use. Popular 1901–22.

Sources: Iowa Seed Company, 1894; Bailey, 1910, p. 1814; Gould, 1974, 4.

Maupay's Superior. Originated with S. Maupay & Company of Philadelphia, by crossing the **Large Red** with the **Fejee** variety. The fruit was of a beautiful deep red color. Above medium size, some of the specimens were quite large. Form round, smooth, seldom corrugated, very solid and heavy. Flesh contained very few seeds and comparatively little water; quite thick through the center and excellent in flavor. The only objectionable characteristics were the extreme delicacy of the skin, which was liable to break or bruise unless handled with great care, and the fruit's tendency to decay very quickly if allowed to mature on the vine. Similar to the **Eureka** and **Foard.**

Sources: *Tilton's Journal of Horticulture* 2 (November 1867): 242, 281–82; Gregory, 1872, 18.

Mayflower. Bright red color; large, splendid, globular shape, slightly flattened, generally smooth. An early variety, ripened uniformly up to the stem. The flesh was solid, free of seeds, and of good flavor. See also **Paragon.**

Sources: *Gardener's Monthly* 25 (July 1883): 205; Livingston's, 1887, 45; Buist, 1890, 103.

May's Favorite (Hawley & Company's). Medium red, uniform, regular fruit.

Sources: *Garden and Forest* 7 (February 14, 1894): 70; *Garden and Forest* 8 (June 26, 1895): 257–58.

Mexican. Large, comparatively smooth, frequently of an oval form, bright red, often tinted with rose or bright pink. Flesh pink, solid, filling the fruit to the center. It was similar to, if not identical with, the **Perfected.**

Source: Burr, 1863, 648.

Mikado (Henderson's). Purplish red color, large, solid, rough, irregular; potato-leafed. Popular 1889–1902. Known as **Turner's Hybrid** before 1891.

Sources: Livingston's, 1887, 45; Bailey, 1887, 24; Bailey, 1910, p. 1816; Gibault, 1912, 376; Uphof, 1959, 222; Gould, 1974, 4.

Mill's Belle. See **Queen.**

Mitchell's Early. Originated in Canada by the same man who developed the **Canada Victor.** Extra early, but the first fruits were inclined to be rough.

Source: Iowa Seed Company, 1894.

Money Maker. Fruit borne in bunches, red, flattened, slightly irregular in form. Elastic character of fruit made it fit for long shipments. Foliage silvery and large. Did well in light sandy soil. See also **Bermuda Extra Early.**

Source: *Landreths' American Grown Seeds,* 1897, 50.

Nellis' Selected Trophy. See **Trophy.**

Nellis' Snowball. See **White Apple.**

New Bay State. Introduced by B. L. Bragg & Company, Springfield, Mass., about 1888. Developed from the old **Trophy** by fifteen years of selection and breeding. Good in flavor, solidity of form, and quality; free of ribs, very little pulp, meaty throughout. Vines hardy but not coarse. Useful for market gardeners, truckers, and farmers.
Source: *Good Housekeeping* 6 (February 18, 1888): vii.

New Cardinal. See **Cardinal** and **Queen.**

New Cluster. Originated with J. C. Ingham of St. Joseph, Mich., in 1865. Introduced by *Prairie Farmer* in 1867. Fruit very solid, not quite so smooth, but without any hardness at the core. Fruit grew in clusters of three to seven tomatoes, ripened by three or four clusters on each lateral. The distance between the clusters was 5–6½ inches.
Source: *Prairie Farmer* 20 (September 21, 1867): 177.

New Giant (Barr & Sugden's). Very large and coarse late variety. Fruit red, very deeply corrugated, and irregular. Plant was robust and not especially prolific.
Source: *Tilton's Journal of Horticulture* 3 (April 1868): 243–44.

New Giant Figi Islands. See **Tilden.**

New Jersey (Thorburn's). Smooth outline, solid flesh. See also **Paragon.**
Source: *Garden and Forest* 2 (September 4, 1889): 432.

New Matchless. See **Matchless.**

New Mexican. New, large, round, apple-shaped; purple color, meaty and productive. Popular in the South because the fruit was better protected by the foliage and hence less liable to be burned by the hot sun. See also **Apple-Shaped.**
Source: Gregory, 1872, 19.

New Peach. See **Peach.**

New Red Apple. See **Excelsior.**

New Stone (Livingston's). Introduced in 1889. Blood red in color, shaped like the **Beauty** and **Favorite.** It was the heaviest for its size, hence its name. A very superior sort, late ripening; producing extraordinarily thick, solid, medium- to large-sized, round, smooth, perfectly uniform, red fruit borne in bunches. Developed from a stock of seed of unknown origin which the introducers obtained from a market gardener near Columbus, Ohio, about 1885. Popular 1893–1936.

Sources: Livingston, 1893, 37; *Landreths' American Grown Seeds,* 1897, 50; Bailey, 1910, pp. 1814, 1816; Boswell, 1938, 21; Gould, 1974, 4.

New Tree. A French variety bearing large red fruit. Grew upright in habit, needing no support to keep the fruit off the ground. See also **French Upright.**

Source: Nellis, 1886, 92.

New Upright. See **French Upright.**

New White Apple. Sweet, with a rich, fruitlike flavor. A cluster variety, just smaller than **Cook's Favorite** in size. See also **White Apple** or **Ivory Ball.**

Source: Gregory, 1872, 19.

New York Early Improved Smooth Red. Found near Philadelphia. After trial, it was preferred to the **Trophy** as a market crop suited to the heavy soils farther north.

Source: *Horticulturist* 26 (November 1871): 342.

New York Market. Fruit bright, light red or yellowish red; smooth, solid; productive. Fruit mostly large and regular, about 4 inches across by 2–2½ inches deep, larger than **Boston Market.** One of the earliest varieties, nearly as early as the **Smooth Red.** In field cultivation ranked next to **Trophy.**

Sources: *Horticulturist* 28 (July 1873): 200; Henderson, 1876, 15; Bailey, 1887, 20.

Nicholson's Hybrid. Earliest variety, recommended for good growing under glass in Boston area.
Sources: *Garden and Forest* 7 (October 24, 1894): 428; *Garden and Forest* 8 (June 26, 1895): 257–58.

Nisbit's Victoria. New English variety, said to have been grown from seeds of Hathaway's **Excelsior.** Pyriform fruit represented to be about the size of a good-sized plum. Fruit almost identical to the **Pear-Shaped,** but the leaves were large and leaflets few, as in the **Mikado.**
Sources: *Gardener's Monthly* 22 (February 1880): 48; Bailey, 1887, 13; Bailey, 1901, 401.

One Hundred Days. See **Hundred Days.**

Optimus. Early; fruit medium-sized, uniform, oval, very smooth, of an exceedingly bright, rich, crimson-scarlet color. Ripened evenly, free from cracks, blemishes, and rotting. Flesh meaty. Vines medium-sized and prolific, bearing fruit in clusters of five. Popular 1885–1911.
Sources: Nellis, 1886, 92; Livingston's, 1887, 45; Iowa Seed Company, 1894; Bailey, 1910, p. 1814; Gould, 1974, 4.

Orangefield. Introduced by Vick from England in 1869. Early, small, round, yellowish red fruit with a sweet, fruity flavor. Fruit rather soft, scarcely angled, nearly as long as broad (about 1½ inches deep in ordinary specimens); often two-celled. Grew in clusters with seven or more specimens in each cluster. When fully ripe, the skin peeled as readily as from an orange. Excellent to eat uncooked. Plant medium in size and growth. Similar to **Dwarf Orangefield, Sim's Mammoth Cherry, Sim's Early Cluster,** and **Large Red Italian.**
Sources: Vick, 1869, 94–95; Gregory, 1872, 18; *Horticulturist* 28 (July 1873): 200; Bailey, 1887, 17.

Orangefield Dwarf. See **Orangefield.**

Paragon (Livingston's). Introduced by Livingston in 1870.

Smooth, large, firm, solid, red or yellowish red fruit; constant in size and shape (3–4 in. across by 2 in. deep). Used by market gardeners and canners. Ripened between the early and late varieties. Popular 1880–97. Similar to the **Arlington, College, Emery, Mayflower, New Jersey, Perfection,** and **Scoville's Hybrid.**

Sources: *Gardener's Monthly* 25 (October 1883): 301; Bailey, 1887, 22; *Landreths' Seed Catalogue,* 1887, 57; Livingston's, 1887, 45; Livingston, 1893, 24–25; *Garden and Forest* 8 (August 21, 1895): 336; *Landreths' American Grown Seeds,* 1897, 50; Gould, 1974, 4.

Peach (Landreth's). Originated in East Tennessee. First marketed by S. Y. Haines of Minneapolis in 1880, who acquired it. Landreth received it from someone in Lynchburg, Va., in 1884 and introduced it the following year. Detached fruit resembled peaches, with red, pinkish, and green blush, sometimes mottled with purple or red purple. Fruit of small or medium size, spherical (1½–2 in. in diameter), very regular and uniform, solid with a rough surface. Flesh red, often two-celled; the juice very dark colored. Fine foliage; vine compact in habit and very productive. Used as novelty and for preserving. Popular 1891–1930.

Sources: *Gardener's Monthly* 29 (December 1887): 369; Bailey, 1887, 22–23; *Landreths' Seed Catalogue,* 1887, 16; *Garden and Forest* 2 (September 4, 1889): 432; Iowa Seed Company, 1894; *Landreths' American Grown Seeds,* 1897, 50; Gould, 1974, 4.

Pear (Henderson's). See **Plum (Red).**

Pear-Shaped (Red). Reddish pink color, small size (1½ in. or less). Firm but tender flesh with few seeds; ripened very slowly. It grew in clusters and derived its name from its shape. Used for stewing, pickling, preserving, and making salads. Popular from 1872 to the present. Also known as **Queen of Tomatoes** and **Poire.** See also **Egg-Shaped.**

Sources: Buist, 1847, 126; *Landreths' Seed Catalogue,* 1859, 18; Thorburn, 1862, 21; *Scientific American,* n. s., 17 (August 3, 1867): 73–74; *Prairie Farmer* 20 (October 5, 1867): 216; W. White, 1868,

APPENDIX 211

313; *Florida Agriculturist* 1 (May 9, 1874): 150–51; Henderson, 1876, 15; Bailey, 1887, 13; *Landreths' Seed Catalogue,* 1887, 57; Gould, 1974, 4.

Pear-Shaped (Yellow). A subvariety of the **Pear-Shaped (Red),** with a clear, semitransparent, yellow skin and yellow flesh. Extraordinarily productive, but little used except for preserving and pickling. Sometimes known as the **Plum (Yellow).**
Sources: Burr, 1863, 652; *Landreths' Seed Catalogue,* 1887, 57.

Perfected. Originated with C. E. Lester about 1860. Pinkish or rose-red color, free from wrinkles or other blemishes. Fruit smooth, large, flattened, solid, and well filled to the center. Flesh firm, thick and pulpy, well flavored, and with few seeds. Plant prolific, vigorous, often attaining a height of 6 or 8 feet and more than 10 feet in good soil. When cooked, it yielded a large return in proportion to its bulk. See also **Fejee.**
Sources: *Homestead* 7 (August 1861): 581; *American Farmer,* 5th ser., 3 (November 1861): 122; Burr, 1863, 648; *Scientific American,* n. s., 17 (August 3, 1867): 74.

Perfection (Livingston's). Introduced by Livingston in 1880. Color was quite distinct: a very glossy crimson with a slight tinge of purple. Fruit elongated and entirely free from ribs; firm, with thick skin and few seeds. It seldom cracked, grew in clusters of four or five large fruits, and retained its very large size late in the season. Used for shipping and early market; adopted by canners because it began to show ripening several days before mature. It was also easy to pick. Popular 1882–1922.
Sources: *American Agriculturist* 41 (March 1882): 126; *Landreths' Seed Catalogue,* 1887, 57; Shaker Seed Company, 1886; Livingston's, 1887, 44; Livingston, 1893, 27; Gould, 1974, 4.

Persian. Whitish yellow in color. Perhaps the **White** variety mentioned by Burr.

Sources: Burr, 1863, 651; *Horticulturist* 28 (July 1873): 200; Bailey, 1887, 20.

Picture Rock. Large uniform size, solid, smooth, of bright scarlet color.
Source: Iowa Seed Company, 1894.

Plum (Red). Bright red or scarlet; solid, oval, symmetrical, uniform size, 1¼–2 inches long by 1 inch in diameter. Flesh pink or rose-red, mild and well flavored with few seeds. Plant was hardy, early, and yielded abundantly. Used for pickling and preserving. Mixed with the **Plum (Yellow)** for a fine garnish or salad. Popular from 1862 to the present.
Sources: Burr, 1863, 649; Henderson, 1867, 218; Bailey, 1887, 14.

Plum (Yellow). Clear, transparent yellow color. Solid, oval, symmetrical, 1¼–2 inches long by 1 inch in diameter. Used for pickling and preserving. Popular from 1862 to the present.
Sources: Thorburn, 1862, 21; Burr, 1863, 652; Gregory, 1872, 19; Henderson, 1876, 15; Bailey, 1887, 14; Gould, 1974, 4.

Poire. See **Pear-Shaped (Red).**

Pomegranate. Originated in Ohio in 1867. Golden-striped fruit, medium size, slightly ridged, and rather flat-shaped. Fruit ripened very early and kept a long time after picking. Vines were rather dwarf and produced abundantly. Named because of similarity to the shape and color of the pomegranate fruit.
Source: *Ohio Farmer* 19 (March 19, 1870): 179.

Pomo d'Oro, Pomo d'Oro Lesteriano, or **Pomo Lesteriano.** See **Perfected.**

Ponderosa. Introduced by Peter Henderson of New York in 1891. Originally named "The Great No. 400," but Henderson had a contest to name the variety and **Ponderosa** won. Mammoth fruit with a purple tinge; not always symmetrical, misshapen, rough, solid as an apple, and with few seeds. Excellent for slicing. Sometimes grew to a weight of 1–2 pounds each. Used for canning and sale to local markets. Popular 1892–1936 and continued to be an important variety through the 1970s.

Sources: Henderson & Company, 1892; *Garden and Forest* 6 (April 26, 1893): 187; *Good Housekeeping* 17 (July 1893): 35; *Landreths' American Grown Seeds,* 1897, 50; Bailey, 1910, pp. 1814, 1816; Gibault, 1912, 376; Uphof, 1959, 222; Gould, 1974, 4.

Potato Leaf (Livingston's). Introduced in 1887. Good-sized, purple fruit with fine flavor; uniform in size, shape and smoothness, and color. Grew in clay. Foliage large-leafed and similar to that of the Irish potato, hence its name. Good for canning whole.

Sources: Bailey, 1887, 24; Livingston, 1893, 35.

Powell's Early. Fruit deep scarlet in color; smooth, round, very solid, with few seeds, and inclined to cluster. Similar to **Large Early Red** and **Tomate Rouge Grosse.**

Sources: Henderson, 1867, 217; Vilmorin-Andrieux, 1885, 568.

Powell's Prolific. See **Large Red.**

Precursor. Large, dark red, less cornered.

Source: Bailey, 1887, 18.

President Garfield. Originated in Germany. Fruit red or yellowish red; large, much doubled and contorted, shapeless and worthless. Similar to **Chiswick Red** and **Prize Belle.** See also **King Humbert** and **Queen.**

Sources: *Gardener's Monthly* 24 (January 1882): 18; Bailey, 1887, 22.

Puritan. Originated in Boston about 1886. Fruit red or yellowish red; large, solid, uniform, slightly angled. Plant large-leafed.

Sources: *Gardener's Monthly* 29 (December 1887): 369; Bailey, 1887, 22; Bailey, 1901, 403.

Prize Belle. See **President Garfield, Queen.**

Queen. Fruit red or yellowish red; firm, uniform, seldom contorted, flattened, slightly lobed, somewhat angled. Ordinary specimens 3 and 4 inches across by 2 inches deep. Popular 1883–90. Similar to the **Queen Mammoth, Cardinal, New Cardinal, Prize Belle, (Livingston's) Favorite, Market Champion, Champion,** and **Mill's Belle.**
Sources: Bailey, 1887, 21; Gould, 1974, 4.

Queen Mammoth. See **Queen.**

Queen of Tomatoes. See **Pear-Shaped (Red).**

Red Apple. See **Apple-Shaped.**

Red Cherry. See **Cherry (Red).**

Red Currant. See **Currant** and **Grape.**

Red Pear-Shaped. See **Pear-Shaped (Red).**

Red Plum. See **Plum (Red).**

Red Valencia Cluster. Red or yellowish red; large, smooth fruit growing in clusters. Fruit somewhat angular, uniform in size and ripening. Similar to the **Queen.**
Sources: Thorburn, 1862, 21; *American Agriculturist* 25 (January 1866): 21; *Prairie Farmer* 20 (October 26, 1867): 262; Bailey, 1887, 21.

Reed's Island Beauty. See **Trophy.**

Rising Sun. Introduced by Mr. Allen about 1871. Large size, round, productive; medium early.
Source: Gregory, 1872, 18.

Rochester or **Rochester Favorite.** See **Acme.**

Roseborough. Similar to **Arlington.**

Rothe Birne. See **Fig-Shaped.**

Rouge Naine Hâtive. See **Early Dwarf Red.**

Round (Red). Small, ovate, roundish, smooth, red variety, measuring about 1 inch in diameter; early and prolific. Used for pickling or preserving.
Sources: Burr, 1863, 649; *Tilton's Journal of Horticulture* 3 (April 1868): 243–44.

Round (Yellow). Small, ovate, roundish, smooth, yellow variety, measuring about 1 inch in diameter; early and prolific. Used for pickling or preserving.
Source: Burr, 1863, 649.

Royal Red (Livingston's). Introduced in 1891. Found among the **Dwarf Champion** fields. Bright scarlet in color. Used for making ketchup. Popular 1893–1907.
Sources: Livingston, 1893, 38; Gould, 1974, 4.

Sacramento Favorite. Originated by George T. Bascom of Sacramento, Calif.
Source: Wickson, 1897, 294.

Salzer's First Prize. Early, flattish, red color, medium size.
Sources: *Garden and Forest* 2 (November 27, 1889): 576; *Garden and Forest* 7 (February 14, 1894): 70.

Santa Catherina. See **Trophy.**

Scoville's Hybrid. Originated by Mr. Scoville as a hybrid of the **Paragon, Trophy,** and **Acme.** See also **Paragon.**
Source: Burpee's, 1888, 22.

Seedless. Rose-red color, solid, and with few seeds. Similar to the **Perfected.**

Sources: Burr, 1863, 650; *General Index*, 1889, 339.

Shah. Yellow or cream-colored fruit; fleshy, thick meat, small seed cavities, grainy and tender in texture and pleasantly mild in flavor. Plant with potato-like leaf. Used for market. Possibly a sport from the **Mikado.**

Sources: Sturtevant, 1889, 42; *Garden and Forest* 6 (April 26, 1893): 187; *Garden and Forest* 8 (April 3, 1895): 138.

Sill's New Funchal. See **Funchal.**

Sim's Early Cluster. Originated by Sims, a gardener to Weedowson, in Dulwich Common, England. Similar to the **Orangefield** and **Round (Red).**

Source: Washburn & Company, 1869, 134–35.

Sim's Mammoth Cherry. See **Orangefield.**

Small Red. See **Cherry (Red).**

Small Yellow. See **Cherry (Yellow).**

Stamfordian. See **Hundred Days.**

Station. Originated at New York Experiment Station as a cross between the **French Upright** and **Alpha.** Small fruit (1½ in. in diameter), nearly regular and uniform in size. An upright plant producing a fruit that began to ripen much earlier than either parent.

Sources: Bailey, 1887, 25; Sturtevant, 1889, 41; *Garden and Forest* 2 (September 4, 1889): 432; Bailey, 1901, 403.

Stone. See **New Stone.**

Striped. See **Gestreifte** and **Golden Striped.**

Sunrise Yellow. See **Golden Queen.**

Sunset. See **Yellow Jefferson.**

Terra Cotta (Thorburn's). Novel red color; medium large, tough, regular fruit.
Source: *Garden and Forest* 7 (February 14, 1894): 70.

Tilden. Discovered in 1858 by Henry Tilden of Davenport, Iowa. Introduced by Apollos W. Harrison of Philadelphia in 1865. Fruit of a deep red color; good, full, moderate size (to a weight of 9 oz.); roundish, varied in form from round to oval, slightly corrugated near the stalk. Liable to rot; core large and hard, resulting in a good deal of waste when the fruit was eaten raw. Plant dwarf, solid and prolific; grew vigorously and yielded abundantly (averaging 60 tomatoes per vine). Leaves deep green. Rather late. Grew in rich soil. Popular 1868–78. Similar to **Lester's Perfected, New Giant Fiji Islands,** and **Red Valencia Cluster.**
Sources: *Prairie Farmer,* n. s., 15 (February 11, 1865): 88; *Prairie Farmer,* n. s., 16 (December 9, 1865): 420; *Tilton's Journal of Horticulture* 1 (February 1866): 99; Henderson, 1867, 217; *Prairie Farmer* 19 (April 23, 1867): 223; *Prairie Farmer* 20 (October 26, 1867): 262; *Gardener's Monthly & Horticultural Advertiser* 10 (January 1868): 10–11; *Tilton's Journal of Horticulture* 3 (April 1868): 243–44; *Landreths' Rural Register,* 1868, 56; *Horticulturist* 23 (November 1868): 321–25; *American Grocer* 2 (May 23, 1870): 231–32; Gregory, 1872, 19; Bailey, 1887, 22; Buist, 1890, 103; *American Gardening* 16 (June 5, 1895): 214–15; Gould, 1974, 4.

Tom Thumb. Clear, light red fruit; firm, meaty, mostly angled, the larger specimens from 2 to 3 inches across and usually less than 1½ inches deep. Early. Dwarf plant (2–2½ feet high); leaflets curled. Similar to **Hundred Days.**
Source: Bailey, 1887, 18.

Tomate à Tige Roide. See **French Upright.**

Tomate de Laye. See **French Upright.**

Tree Tomato. See **French Upright.**

Tree Tomato à Tige Roide. See **French Upright** and **Station.**

Triumph. Hybrid of a wild variety found on the Brazos, in Texas, and the **Tilden.** Early. Popular 1879–80.
    Sources: *Prairie Farmer* 44 (April 19, 1873): 122; Gould, 1974, 4.

Trophy. Breeding began in the mid-1840s. Introduced after the Civil War by Col. George E. Waring of Newport, R. I. Deep, dark red fruit contrasting with green foliage. Large size, smooth, solid; good flavor, fleshy, few seeds; flattish, about 4 or 5 inches across by 2½ inches deep. Exceedingly liable to grow too large and irregular. Waring initially sold seeds for 25 cents apiece. One tomato, not the largest on the vines, measured 16 inches in circumference. Vines were vigorous growers and enormous bearers. Fruit ripened badly around the stem and burst in bad weather. Its tendency to remain a little green near the stem may have affected its value in some localities. Used as a fresh tomato and for canning. Popular 1872–1926. Similar to **Blounts' Champion Cluster, Buist's Selected Trophy, Henderson's Extra Selected Trophy, Island Beauty, Nellis' Selected Trophy, Reed's Island Beauty,** and **Santa Catherina.**
    Sources: *American Agriculturist* 28 (October 1869): 362; *Horticulturist* 25 (February 1870): 51; *American Agriculturist* 30 (May 1871): 207; *Horticulturist* 26 (May 1871): 159; *Practical Farmer* 8 (May 1871): 116; *American Agriculturist* 30 (July 1871): 266; *Horticulturist* 26 (November 1871): 342; Gregory, 1872, 6; *Landreths' Rural Register,* 1872, 64; *American Agriculturist* 32 (April 1873): 144; *Prairie Farmer* 44 (April 19, 1873): 122; *American Farmer,* 8th ser., 3 (December 1873): 422–23; *Horticulturist* 29 (June 1874): 178; *American Agriculturist* 41 (April 1882): 160; *Gardener's Monthly* 25 (July 1883): 205; *Gardener's Monthly* 25 (October 1883): 301; Bailey, 1887, 20–21; *Garden and Forest* 2 (November 27, 1889): 576; Gould, 1974, 4.

TTT or Ten Ton Tomato. Fruit deep red; large, round, half flat, smooth, solid, free from green core or other imperfections; in form

slightly flattened at both stem and blossom ends. Fruit cut across or transversely revealed a solid meaty interior, free from air spaces or hard core. Yielded twenty thousand pounds or ten tons to the acre. Used by canners.
Source: *Landreths' American Grown Seeds,* 1897, 50.

Turban. See **Turk's Cap.**

Turkesbund. See **Turk's Cap.**

Turk's Cap. Originated in Germany. Medium-sized fruit with a peculiar and agreeable flavor; 1½–2 inches across, nearly spherical, crowned by a singular, irregular mass of protruded, fleshy cells. It was borne in large clusters, in a form vaguely reminiscent of a turban. Plants produced many slender, upright shoots. Valuable only as a curiosity. Popular 1880–82. Also known as **Turkesbund** or **Turk's Turban.**
Sources: *Gardener's Monthly* 22 (March 1880): 81; Bailey, 1887, 18; Gould, 1974, 4.

Turner Hybrid. Introduced by Burpee in 1885. Fruit deep brilliant red color; smooth, solid, about 4–6 inches in diameter and 12–24 ounces in weight; fine flavor. Large leaves were entire and not cut. Strong and productive grower. Popular 1885–91. Renamed **Mikado** in 1891. See also **Potato Leaf** and **Mikado.**
Sources: *Gardener's Monthly* 28 (March 1886): 80; Livingston's, 1887, 45; Burpee's, 1888, 22; Gould, 1974, 4.

Turner's Hybrid. Originated by Mr. Turner of Norwich, Conn.; a hybrid between **Keyes' Early Prolific** and **Crimson Cluster.** Introduced by Peter Henderson about 1870. Early, solid, seedless, small- to medium-sized, thick skinned. Productive, yielding from twenty to thirty fruits in a cluster. Used for shipping purposes.
Source: *American Agriculturist* 30 (December 1871): 460.

Valencia Cluster. See **Red Valencia Cluster.**

Validum. See **French Upright.**

Virginia Corker. Red fruit; large size, heavy, thick, and meaty; productive. Used by market gardeners.
Source: *Landreths' American Grown Seeds,* 1897, np.

White. See **Persian.**

White or **Straw Colored.** If screened by foliage or grown in the shade, fruit was almost clear white; if exposed to the sun, it assumed a pale, yellowish tinge. Fruit large, generally ribbed, often irregular, but sometimes smooth. Flesh yellowish, watery, with a peculiar flavor esteemed by some but unpalatable to others. The variety was hardy, productive, and early; but its color, before and after being cooked, was unattractive. It was rarely seen in the markets and seldom cultivated for family use. See also **Persian.**
Source: Burr, 1863, 651.

White Apple. Fruit nearly white in color; small and spherical, occasionally somewhat irregular in shape, 1 or 1½ inches in diameter; soft flesh, often two-celled. Valuable only as a curiosity. Used for salads and making pickles. Popular 1887–1930. Similar to or same as **New White Apple, Nellis' Snowball, Ivory Ball,** and **Apfel Weisser.**
Sources: *Florida Agriculturist* 1 (May 9, 1874): 150–51; Bailey, 1887, 19; Gould, 1974, 4.

White's Extra Early. Early, medium-sized variety of a deep red color. Generally round and comparatively smooth, but frequently of an oval form, flattened and sometimes ribbed. Average specimens measured about 2½ inches in diameter by 1½ inches in depth. Flesh was pale red, firm, mild, with few seeds. When cooked, it yielded much pulp of good quality. The plants were moderately vigorous and easily distinguished by their peculiar curled and apparently withering foliage.
Source: Burr, 1865, 641.

Wonder of Italy. See **Fig-Shaped.**

Yellow Cherry. See **Cherry (Yellow).**

Yellow Fig. See **Fig (Yellow).**

Yellow Jefferson. Bright yellow in color, often with a red cheek. Rounder than **Golden Queen,** not inclined to become angular, strongly resembling a **Paragon.** Also called **Sunset.**
Source: Bailey, 1887, 20.

Yellow Pear-Shaped. See **Pear-Shaped (Yellow).**

Yellow Plum. See **Plum (Yellow).**

Yellow Trophy. Golden yellow, apple-shaped fruit. The skins of some specimens had a metallic luster. Thin septa, tough flesh, with large and abundant seeds.
Source: *Garden and Forest* 8 (April 3, 1895): 138.

Yellow Victor. See **Golden Trophy.**

BIBLIOGRAPHY

BOOKS AND PAMPHLETS

Anderson, James, ed. 1874. *New Practical Gardener and Modern Horticulturist.* London: W. Mackenzie.
Bailey, Liberty Hyde. 1886. "Notes on Tomatoes." Agricultural College of Michigan *Bulletin* No. 19. Lansing: Thorp & Godfrey.
————. 1887. "Notes on Tomatoes." Agricultural College of Michigan *Bulletin* No. 31. Lansing: Thorp & Godfrey State Printers and Binders.
————. 1901. *The Principles of Vegetable-gardening.* New York: Macmillan Company.

222   APPENDIX

────────. 1910. *Cyclopedia of American Horticulture.* 4 vols. New York: Macmillan Company.

Benson, Albert Emerson. 1929. *History of the Massachusetts Horticultural Society.* Norwood, Mass.: Plimpton Press.

Boswell, Victor R. 1938. "Improvement and Genetics of Tomatoes, Peppers, and Eggplant." U.S. Department of Agriculture's *Yearbook, 1937.* Washington, D.C.: U.S.D.A.

Buist, Robert. 1847. *The Family Kitchen Gardener.* New York: J. C. Riker.

Burr, Fearing. 1863. *The Field and Garden Vegetables of America.* Boston: Crosby and Nichols.

────────. 1865. *The Field and Garden Vegetables of America.* Boston: J. E. Tilton.

Day, J. W. 1891. *A Treatise on Tomato Culture.* Crystal Springs, Miss.: By the author.

General Index of Michigan Agricultural Reports, Including the Transactions of the State Agricultural Society 1849–1859, and the Annual Reports of the State Board of Agriculture, 1862–1888. 1889. Lansing: Darius D. Thorp, State Printer.

Gibault, Georges. 1912. *Histoire des légumes.* Paris: Libraire Horticole.

Goodholme, Todd S. 1877. *A Domestic Cyclopedia of Practical Information.* New York: Henry Holt and Company.

Gould, Wilbur. 1974. *Tomato Production, Processing and Quality Evaluation.* Westport, Conn.: AVI Publishing Company.

Hedrick, U. P., ed. 1919. *Sturtevant's Edible Plants of the World.* Reprint, New York: Dover, 1972.

Henderson, Peter. 1867. *Gardening for Profit; A Guide to the Successful Cultivation of the Market and Family Garden.* New York: Orange Judd.

Klose, Nelson. 1950. *America's Crop Heritage: The History of Foreign Plant Introduction by the Federal Government.* Ames: Iowa State College Press.

Livingston, A. W. 1893. *Livingston and the Tomato.* Columbus, Ohio: A. W. Livingston's Sons.

Manning, Robert. 1880. *History of the Massachusetts Horticultural Society 1829–1878.* Boston: Rand, Avery & Company.

Morrison, Gordon. 1838. "Tomato Varieties." Agricultural Experiment Station Special *Bulletin* No. 290. East Lansing: Michigan State College, April.

Munson, Welton M. 1893. *Annual Report of the Maine State College for the Year 1893.* Part II. Augusta: Burleigh and Flynt.

Nicholson, George, ed. 1887. *The Illustrated Dictionary of Gardening, A Practical and Scientific Encyclopedia of Horticulture for Gardeners and Botanists.* Division VII.—Sel to Zyg. London: L. Upcott Gill.

Parkinson, Cornelia. 1985. *Alex Livingston: The Tomato Man, 1821–1898.* Reynoldsburg, Ohio: Published by the author.

————. 1996. *Alex Livingston: The Tomato Man and His Times.* Reynoldsburg, Ohio: Historical Tales Ink.

Root, A. I., J. W. Day, and D. Cummins. 1892 (2d ed. 1906). *Tomato Culture.* Medina, Ohio: A. I. Root Company.

Smith, Andrew F. 1994. *The Tomato in America: Early History, Culture and Cookery.* Columbia: University of South Carolina Press.

Smith, F. F. 1876. *Tomatoes from Seed to the Table.* Aurora, Ill.: Knickerbocker & Hodder.

Sturtevant, E. Lewis. 1889. "The Tomato." Maryland Agricultural Experiment Station *Special Bulletin,* 18–25.

Tomato Facts: The Story of the Evolution of the Tomato. 1909. Columbus, Ohio: Livingston Seed Company.

Tracy, Will. 1907. *Tomato Culture.* New York: Orange Judd.

Uphof, J. C. 1959. *Dictionary of Economic Plants.* New York: Hafner Publishing Co.

U.S. Department of Agriculture. 1875. *Report of the Commissioner of Agriculture for the Year 1874.* Washington, D.C.: Government Printing Office.

Vilmorin-Andrieux, MM. 1885. *The Vegetable Garden: Illustrations, Descriptions, and Culture of the Garden Vegetables of Cold and Temperate Climates.* Translated by William Miller. London: J. Murray. Reprint, Berkeley, Calif.: Ten Speed Press, 1981.

White, William. 1868. *Gardening for the South, or How to Grow Vegetables and Fruits.* Rev. and Newly Stereotyped. New York: Orange Judd.

Wickson, Edward J. 1897. *The California Vegetables in Garden and Field.* San Francisco: Pacific Rural Press.

Work, Paul. 1947. *The Tomato.* New York: Orange Judd.

SEED CATALOGUES

Booth, William. 1810. *A Catalogue of Kitchen Garden Seeds and Plants.* Baltimore: G. Dobbin and Murphy.

Buist, Robert. 1859. *Buist's Almanac and Garden Manual.* Philadelphia: King & Baird.

————. 1863. *Gardeners', Planters', and Farmers' Priced Catalogue of Buist's Genuine Garden Seeds.* Philadelphia: King & Baird.

————. 1890. *Buist's Garden Guide and Almanac.* Philadelphia.

Burdick & Barrett. 1857. *Catalog of Seeds and Agricultural Implements.* Providence, R.I.: Knowles, Anthony & Company.

Burpee, W. Atlee, & Company. 1880. "The Matchless Tomato." Philadelphia. Broadside.

————. 1888. *Burpee's Farm Annual; Garden, Farm & Flower Seeds.* Philadelphia.

Comstock, Ferre & Company. 1849. "Catalogue of Garden Seeds." Wethersfield, Conn. Broadside.

————. 1852 and 1853. *Descriptive Catalogue of Garden Seeds.* Wethersfield, Conn.

Dreer, Henry A. 1864 and 1872. *Dreer's Garden Calendar.* Philadelphia.

Dunlap & Thomsom. 1847. *Catalogue of Seeds, Roots, and Shrubs.* New York: J. W. Bell.

Elliott & Company. 1855. *Catalogue of Agricultural and Horticultural Implements and Machines, Garden Field and Flower Seeds, Fruit & Ornamental Trees.* Cleveland, Ohio: Harris, Fairbanks & Company.

Garden Seed Crop of 1850 Raised at South Union, Ky. Shakertown, South Union, Kentucky. Broadside.

Gregory, James J. H. 1872. *James J. H. Gregory's Seed Circular and Retail Catalogue*. Marblehead, Mass.: Pease, Traill & Fielden.

Henderson, Peter. 1876. *Peter Henderson's & Company: Abridged List of Everything for the Garden*. New York.

Henderson, Peter, & Company. 1892. *Catalogue*. New York.

Iowa Seed Company. 1894. *1894 Collection*. Des Moines, Iowa.

Kozolowski, Otto. 1898. *Farmer Seed Co, Farmers and Seed Growers*. Faribault, Minn.

Landreth, David, and Cuthbert Landreth. 1849. *Seed Catalogue*. Philadelphia.

Landreths' American Grown Seeds. 1897. Bristol, Penn.

Landreths' Rural Register and Almanac. 1868. Philadelphia.

————. 1872. Philadelphia.

————. 1876. Philadelphia.

Landreths' Seed Catalogue. 1859 and 1887. Philadelphia: Landreth Seed Company.

Livingston's, A. W., Sons. 1887. *Livingston's Seed Annual*. Columbus, Ohio.

McCullough, J. M., & Son. 1858. *Catalogue of Fruit and Ornamental Trees, Shrubs, Plants, Vines & Roses*. Cincinnati: Wrightson & Company.

————. 1890. *Annual Seed Catalogue*. Cincinnati, Ohio.

Nellis, A. C., Company. 1884 and 1886. *Nellis' Floral and Garden Instructor*. Canajoharie, N.Y.

Price & Reed. 1890. *The Albany Seed Store*. Albany, N. Y. Catalogue.

Prouty, David, and Company. 1851. *Catalogue of Garden, Flower, Field and Grass Seeds, & c*. Boston.

Root, A. I. 1895. *Catalog of Seeds for the Greenhouse, Garden and Farmer, 1886–1895*. 18th ed. Medina, Ohio, April 1.

Schlegel, Everett, & Co. 1878. *Retail Price-list and Catalogue of Seeds*. Boston: Thomas Todd.

Shaker Seed Company. 1886. Mt. Lebanon, N. Y. Broadside.

Strong, B. N., & Company. 1852. *American Seed Garden*. Wethersfield, Conn.: Elisha Johnson, A. W. Robbins, E. G. Robbins, W. Adams.

Thorburn, James M., & Company. 1844 and 1862. *Annual Catalogue.* New York: Isaac J. Oliver.

Vick, James. 1869. *Illustrated Catalogue and Floral Guide for 1869.* Rochester, N.Y.

————. 1871. *Vick's Floral Guide for 1871.* Rochester, N.Y.

Warren's Garden and Nursery. 1845–46. *Annual Descriptive Catalogue of Fruit and Ornamental Trees.* Boston.

Washburn & Company. 1869. *Amateur Cultivator's Guide to the Flower and Kitchen Garden.* Boston, Mass.: Washburn and Company.

White, Jefferson. 1852. *The Gardener's Manual.* Thompsonville, Conn.

WHERE TO GET HEIRLOOM TOMATO SEEDS

Seed Savers Exchange
3076 North Winn Road
Decorah, IA 52101
(319) 382-5990

Southern Exposure Seed Exchange
P.O. Box 170
Earlysville, VA 22959
(804) 973-4703

Tomato Growers Supply Company
P.O. Box 2237
Fort Myers, FL 33902
(941) 768-1119

Totally Tomatoes
P.O. Box 1626
Augusta, GA 30903
(803) 663-0016